Praise for
When God Waits

"Jerome Daley explains the value of faithfully doing what we know to do until God reveals the next step. None of us likes to wait. But God does some of his most important work in the lives of those who are waiting for God to fulfill the calling he has placed on them. If you're longing for God to open up your destiny, read this book. *When God Waits* is a much-needed gift to all who have ever wished that God would just hurry up!"

—TED HAGGARD, pastor, author, and president of the
National Association of Evangelicals

"In *When God Waits,* Jerome Daley probes one of God's more frustrating habits: promising a hope and a future, and then hanging fire. What is God waiting for? Daley, in search of an answer, quarries several stories from Scripture as well as his own season of limbo and emerges with a reminder of the riches hidden within divine delay."

—MARK BUCHANAN, author of *The Holy Wild*

"Jerome Daley reminds us of the beauty, presence, and purpose of God in the waiting period and that God is just as amazing then as he is at any other time. Readers will grow to trust God even more and will be greatly rewarded as they are encouraged to faint not."

—CHE AHN, senior pastor, Ha rvest Rock Church,
Pasadena, California

"*When God Waits* provides a landing place for the confusion and disillusionment that come from seasons of seeming inactivity on the part of God. Jerome Daley has done my heart a service through this beautiful work, encouraging me that the waiting is actually doing something in me, is actually taking me somewhere good."

—JAN MEYERS, author of *The Allure of Hope*
and *Listening to Love*

"Jerome Daley has extended an irresistible invitation to those of us who sometimes find ourselves desperately clinging to the hope that there's a purpose in life's disappointments and difficulties. *When God Waits* is written by someone who, having endured the darkness, has become resolute in his belief that God is unrelentingly good and outrageously in love with us."

—FIL ANDERSON, author of *Running on Empty:*
Contemplative Spirituality for Overachievers

"Even when our lives seem chaotic and aimless, God is up to something. *When God Waits* gives us fresh insight to liberate us from discouragement and confusion when things don't appear to work out the way we want. Even more, it gives us a strategic plan of action to follow that will lead to activating the destiny God has for us."

—LINUS MORRIS, president, Christian Associates
International

When God

Waits

making

sense

of

divine

delays

Jerome Daley

WaterBrook
PRESS

WHEN GOD WAITS
PUBLISHED BY WATERBROOK PRESS
2375 Telstar Drive, Suite 160
Colorado Springs, Colorado 80920
A division of Random House, Inc.

ISBN 1-57856-895-1

Library of Congress Cataloging-in-Publication Data
Daley, Jerome.
    When God waits : making sense of divine delays / Jerome Daley.— 1st ed.
        p. cm.
    Includes bibliographical references.
    ISBN 1-57856-895-1
    1. Patience—Religious aspects—Christianity. I. Title.
    BV4647.P3.D35 2005
    241'.4—dc22

                                                            2004024536

Printed in the United States of America
2005—First Edition

10 9 8 7 6 5 4 3 2 1

This book is dedicated to pilgrims everywhere,
to those who have chosen a life of pursuit
and obtained the rewards of waiting...

Yours is a rich destiny.

Contents

Acknowledgments

The journey of life may be lonely at times but never solitary. Neither is the journey of writing a book. Both my life and writing have been deeply enriched by many people who in various ways have shared our waiting season and our reach for the destiny of intimacy.

The mad conquest of my life would be impossible if not for the unflagging commitment and strength of my co-conspirator and adventurous dreamer—my wife, Kellie. Your love and partnership are my greatest treasure. I also cherish the treasure of my three children: Abigail, Ashley, and Thorpe. You have helped me learn to savor the sweet opportunities in seasons of waiting!

In our vision for true friendship and community, God has bound Kellie and me uniquely to two courageous souls: Paige and Paul Jobe. Thank you for taking the wild ride with us and helping us wait well. In addition, we want to recognize the brothers and sisters of our annual Wilder Weekend and its contribution to our growth in community.

Special thanks go to several friends who offered warm encouragement and insight with the manuscript—Mark and Esther Maltby, Tucker and Denise Ritner, and Fil Anderson. Mark, our Thursday mornings together have been irreplaceable.

To our pastor, Rodney Odom, and his wife, Marcia, thank you for offering us your acceptance, mentoring, and friendship. Your servant leadership has provided a unique combination of safety and freedom to pursue the fullness of the Kingdom.

I am also deeply grateful for the vision and assistance of those who transformed this message into a book: my publisher, Don Pape; my agent, Steve Laube; and my editor, Ron Lee.

Hope deferred makes the heart sick,
but a longing fulfilled is a tree of life.

—Proverbs 13:12

An Invitation to Intimacy

Four years ago I suddenly resigned my position as worship pastor at a North Carolina church and moved my family to Colorado for a year's Sabbatical in the Rocky Mountains. This move was precipitated by a mounting inner crisis—a crisis of soul, a crisis of spirit, and a crisis of marriage. My life felt like it was coming unglued. My hands were full of random pieces, but I didn't know where they belonged.

Thus began the hardest—and best—year of my life as God began to reveal his blueprints of identity and destiny to my wife, Kellie, and me. After completing that stage of the journey (and writing it into a book), we returned to our home state with our three children, two cats, and very high hopes.[1] This is where our current story begins…and where our season of waiting begins as well.

In my experience, waiting is some of the hardest "work" we get to do. But if it is not merely we but God who initiates this waiting, then deep purpose resides here! My hope in this book is to tap into these purposes and make sense of their effects upon our lives. Ultimately, I am convinced that *waiting is an invitation to intimacy*…an invitation we can embrace or ignore. Let us together embrace it and come to know him as never before.

Before I launch into our story, I'd like to toss an idea at you. I'm not usually a fan of Christian T-shirts. They are typically trite, culturally irrelevant, and poorly designed. But in the early 1990s there was a T-shirt that proclaimed a bold truth: "Life is hard. God is good. Let's dance!"

Succinct but not trite. And it's all there; everything we really need to know about life and destiny is captured in kernel in this pithy declaration. The sum of our lives…and the sum of this book…is the exploration of those very truths.

This book is about the unrelenting goodness of God in the face of great hardness. It's about a passionate intimacy with God that is forged in the fires of waiting.

If there's one ongoing misemphasis in the Christian world, it's a persistent preoccupation with *principles* at the expense of the *Person*. Christians like lessons that are concrete: biblical keys to surviving the desert or seven steps to discovering your personal destiny. Principles are clean, neat, straightforward, and reassuring. We dissect a biblical hero, perhaps even Jesus, and then distill a set of principles from that person's life and apply it to the entire Christian populace in a one-size-fits-all fashion. But there's more than a hint of a "Job's friends" mentality in such an exercise, which should give us all second thoughts about embracing principles and missing the Person.

When the godly man Job encountered tragedy upon tragedy,

his friends could point only to principles and then conclude that Job must certainly be bearing the judgment that his sins deserved. And yet, after God had broken into the conversation and the dust had cleared, the honesty and authenticity of Job's relationship with God found greater favor than his buddies' principles—even the true ones.[2]

Yes, there is a collection of timeless truths that frame the lives of Christ followers. But these *principles,* if you will, merely form the border of the painting—the structure that allows us to view the creative uniqueness of the painting itself.

Why do I bring up this interplay between *principle* and *Person?* Because the correct focus will sustain us when we're caught in a season of waiting, when our destiny feels out of reach. When we're desperate, despondent, doubting, that's when we don't need another list of principles. We need Jesus himself. Principles are powerful allies, particularly in keeping you from doing stupid things like releasing your frustration on the gambling table or in an extramarital affair. But it's only the divine Presence that stills the echoes of abandonment that arise as dark whispers in dark moments.

And it's the whispered strategies from the mouth of this Presence that we need in order to wait well. At the end of each chapter that follows, I have recapped the waiting strategy for that chapter through the actual experience of a biblical man or woman. Then I have provided journaling space for your personal interaction with God related to that strategy. Even if you don't like to write, let me encourage you to write in this book. The act of picking up a pen and capturing your inner musings on paper is powerfully redemptive. It's a way of owning and personalizing these truths into your unique journey. Incorporate your prayers and questions, revelations and frustrations in this section.

I invite you to journey with me into both the hardness of life and the goodness of God, further than either of us has dared venture before. It is my greatest hope that we will come face to face with the kindest and most fearsome Person I know...and be captivated by his passion for us!

Chapter One

Why All This Waiting?

Destiny and the Weakness of Waiting

> Being fully present in the now
> is perhaps the premiere skill
> of the spiritual life.
> —BRENNAN MANNING[1]

My face was getting tired of holding the smile in place. Kellie and I were visiting friends at a North Carolina beach, and we found ourselves reciting, once again, the reasons why we believed God had brought us back to the Southeast from Colorado. The reasons weren't complicated. We now had an opportunity to build a new ministry. To partner with a new church. To build community with new friends.

We had returned to North Carolina believing this was God's clear leading, but the tale was starting to wear thin. As I spoke the words to our friends, I wondered whom I was trying to convince. I'd been buffing this vision with the cloth of conversation, trying to make the jewel shine as brightly as it had months earlier. Was I still trying to talk *myself* into this grandiose vision?

Kellie and I returned to our home state from a surreal sabbatical in Colorado Springs. We'd come down from the mountaintop, as it were, to bring our rediscovered souls, family, and God back into a newly commissioned assignment of ministry in Greensboro, North Carolina. It was time, we knew deep in our hearts, to release our revitalized *being* into a new kind of *doing*. With the insights we'd gained during the previous two years, we looked forward to a ministry free of the frenzied and fragmented strivings of years past. Instead, we were eager to enjoy the overflow of God's lavish presence, drawing deeply from his unceasing goodness and living securely and satisfied in him alone.

We both knew God had given us fragments of purpose, direction we could trust, but still we felt subterranean tremors of uncertainty: *can we do this?* The luster of the dream was fading slightly as we confronted the dank reality of this new place: No ministry. No church. No ministry partners. And precious few friends.

It was inevitable, of course, that we would have to field the looming question time and again: "So, what are you doing now that you're back from Colorado?" I realize that normal people have perfectly convincing, validating answers to this question. And then there was me. I vacillated between seeing myself as Spaceman Spiff, the intrepid explorer charting undiscovered territories, and a rather worse-for-wear jack-in-the-box on the island of misfit toys. Kellie and I were calling our new venture oneFlesh Ministries, and it was our burning desire to write, speak, and lead worship for the purpose of drawing people into greater intimacy with God and one another. But how would we fulfill this dream? How does a person step into destiny? I was tired of offering vague answers to the constant questions.

Our beach friends were gracious and supportive; they knew about launching out on a dream, having moved across the state not long before to pastor a church plant in this coastal community. But as I worked to maintain my confident smile while talking about the future, my soul was being rocked by waves of doubt and fear. Could I really afford to gamble my future on a dream?

And why wasn't it coming together? My first book, *Soul Space*, wouldn't be released for another six months. Our savings were gone, and our income was nil. *Who am I kidding, telling our friends about this dream, this fantasy called oneFlesh Ministries? Kidding myself probably.*

Our vision had been birthed during a year in the stunning foothills of the Rocky Mountains. We had remained a second year to write down the soulquaking discoveries we'd made, to turn those insights into a book. The waiting really began that second year, as we wrote and hoped, prayed and dreamed about what God was making us to be and do.

Since we had taken the plunge to return back east in the summer of 2002, the onus was suddenly on us to put up or shut up, to make good on all our talk about ramping into a new ministry or just bag it and get a "real job." So far, nothing was happening. Why do transitions have to be so ambiguous? Couldn't this just be simple and straightforward for a change? But often, it seems, transition demands that we relinquish the old before the new can take tangible form. If that's true, then maybe this weightless, unanchored in-betweenness is what transition is all about. Maybe, despite the discomfort, there is purpose in waiting. At least we hoped so.

The Weakness of Waiting

Waiting. I don't like it…that much I have decided. Waiting feels so passive. So impotent. Waiting feels indecisive and irresponsible.

More to the point, waiting feels weak…and I definitely don't like weak. However, our journey in God frequently involves the weakness of waiting. Can you relate to that? Does it feel as though you're waiting for someone to hit the button and take your life off Pause? Does your destiny seem to hang out there, clearly visible but remaining just beyond your reach?

Months back I was pondering the rather staggering waiting season that my favorite biblical hero, David, endured. The prophet Samuel had already anointed David king of Israel, but he was nowhere near the throne. Not only was David's reign over Israel not seeming to move toward reality, but all indications were just the opposite. King Saul was doing his best to kill the shepherd boy who posed such a threat merely because he was breathing. Gradually it began to dawn on me that David was not an aberration. With a mixture of fascination and dread, I began to review the stories of various biblical leaders—the movers and shakers we go to for inspiration. And guess what I found? Almost every man or woman whose story wound up in the Bible spent significant years doing one thing: waiting!

I'm not talking about waiting for the time they would be called to leadership. These people had *already* received God's call, the dream was in place, the vision had been cast. But still they had to wait—*after* God had spoken a purpose or destiny for their lives. To all outward appearances, nothing was happening. Or in David's case, his life had been a lot easier *before* God decided to name him the next king of Israel.

As much as I resist this idea, there appears to be a defining pattern in the plan of God: waiting necessarily precedes fulfillment. I'd love to be wrong on this, but I am becoming more convinced that waiting is inescapable. Waiting 101 is the prerequisite class for Intermediate Ministry, and often Waiting 201 comes before Advanced Serving. And I'm not talking about only those who are called to full-time Christian service. I'm talking about people called to full-time living! Living successfully in the Kingdom of God requires mastering the rare art of waiting well.

HEROES IN THE ART OF WAITING

Consider some of the heroes in Scripture who didn't do a whole lot other than wait before they realized their destiny:

LEADER	CALLING	SEASON(S) OF WAITING
Abraham	father to a nation	25 years
Joseph	leader of a nation	13 years + 10 more
Moses	deliverer of a nation	40 years + 40 more
David	king of a nation	about 17 years + 7.5 more[2]
Joshua and Zerubbabel	rebuilders of a nation	20 years
John the Baptist	forerunner of Messiah	1–2 years
Mary	mother of the Messiah	33 years
Paul	witness to the Messiah	3 years

Do those numbers surprise you as much as they did me? Time after time God drops a word of tremendous destiny into the hearts of his people and then does…nothing! *God, what could you be thinking?!* The calling hangs out there, tantalizing, wonderful, visible but just out of reach, and this goes on for years and years. And then, when hope is extruded to a brittle filament, stripped to just one tempered thread of tenacious conviction, fulfillment comes.

Not convinced yet? All right, let's look at more examples.

LEADER	CALLING	SEASON(S) OF WAITING
Noah	salvation from Flood	2–5 years[3]
Jacob	return to his homeland	20 years
Joshua and Caleb	conquer Canaan	45 years + 2–5 more

Leader	Calling	Season(s) of Waiting
Hannah	have a child	5–15 years[4]
Esther	salvation for a nation	about 5 years[5]
Simeon and Anna	testify to Christ	many years
Jesus	salvation for the world	18 years[6]

Dare We Still Dream?

Are you caught in that long season of waiting? Are you struggling to get into gear so you can pursue what you were made for? Be encouraged: time spent in the weakness of waiting is time that God uses to forge the soul of destiny. It is rare that God's people stumble into seasons of anointing and purpose without first enduring a great deal of preparation. It's more true and much more common that God's people first do a lot of waiting. These are the people God raises up to instigate renewal and action.

God wants us to fully experience the weakness of waiting. And in the midst of this waiting, God offers a word of hope: "[Don't] become weary in doing good, for at the proper time [you] will reap a harvest if [you] do not give up" (Galatians 6:9). Can you receive that promise into your current place in life? I encourage you to pause right now, close your eyes, and let that word of truth wash over you.

Perhaps you don't see yourself as a commissioned hero, not a great leader like the biblical men and women I listed earlier. Maybe your sense of calling seems very small—to raise children, to make a career, to know Jesus better, to serve in the church. Whatever your calling, the dreams that God plants inside you are powerful for the Kingdom of God! And they are yours to be stewarded well.

When I was in college, my friend Jeff used to talk about being a world changer. He said he knew deep down that he was supposed to accomplish big things for God. I admired the overarching sense of leadership that he felt, but I couldn't relate. Jeff was charismatic, winsome, and likable—a natural leader. In contrast, my world felt comfortably small and known. My ambitions didn't rise much above having good friends, encouraging people to know God, and playing in a worship band. To be honest, they still don't! But I'm learning to dream, learning to believe that what God has begun, he will finish in my life. And in yours.

THE GIFT OF DESTINY

When it comes to dreams, there are those few people who reach for the stars. The rest of us are mostly afraid. Afraid to dream, afraid to take risks, afraid to fail and make a fool of ourselves. It feels much safer to go with the flow, to set ordinary goals that we can reach by ordinary means. But like it or not, we were made for more. God designed us for both agonies and thrills, defeats and victories.

Henri Nouwen in his book *Can You Drink the Cup?* reflects on sacred moments around his table as he was growing up, when his father would ceremoniously lift a glass of wine to toast family and guests. Looking back at the impression those times made upon his soul, Nouwen says this:

> Lifting up the cup is an invitation to affirm and celebrate life together. As we lift up the cup of life and look each other in the eye, we say: "Let's not be anxious or afraid. Let's hold our cup together and greet each other. Let us not hesitate to acknowledge the reality of our lives and encourage each other to be grateful for the gifts we have received."[7]

Whether we realize it or not, God has given us the gift of destiny—every one of us. That destiny may be quiet and unnoticed by others, or it may be center stage in the public arena. But one thing is certain: laying hold of our destiny is vital to the interests of God and the satisfaction of our souls.

The lofty concept of destiny probably feels far removed from the mundane normalcy of your daily life. It often does from mine. But that feeling is a deception; destiny begins now. Until we accept and hold close our God-breathed vision for life and bring it into today, it remains lost in an unattainable future netherworld. This is why I quoted Brennan Manning's bold statement at the beginning of this chapter: "Being fully present in the now is perhaps the premiere skill of the spiritual life."[8] Compared to all the other outstanding Christian disciplines and skills—prayer, meditation, fasting, study, silence, solitude, and so forth—it seems arrogant at best to elevate this highly intangible goal above the rest.

Nevertheless, over the years I have spent much time contemplating Manning's statement, and its potent truth is gently illuminating my soul. The grace to live fully and completely in *today* brings explosive transformation to our seasons of waiting. <u>Awakening to the full potential of now releases strength from the weakness of waiting. Suddenly, waiting is not a barrier to destiny but the means of it. Waiting is not an enemy to be conquered but a friend to be embraced.</u> Waiting is bursting with potential, overflowing with the abundance of God himself! This call to embrace the now is a divine strategy for unwrapping the gift of waiting and discovering its unique purpose in your journey.

Strategy No. 1:

Embrace the now.

In addition to embracing the now, nine other strategies elevate waiting to its rightful place among the spiritual disciplines. In each of the following chapters, we will look at a different strategy to harness your waiting season toward destiny.

Destiny was on my mind a couple of nights ago when I was invited by a Christian comedian to watch him put on a show for youth on the topic of sexual abstinence. As the lights dimmed and the music for *Mission: Impossible* rolled across the church auditorium, the spotlight followed a bald man in jeans and a T-shirt jogging up the aisle and leaping onto the stage. With the energy of a teenager, this thirty-something guy bounded around the room, walked over chairs, threatened, smirked, snorted, deadpanned, and harassed everyone in the house. But ultimately he kept kids and parents alike laughing and thinking for the better part of ninety minutes.

It was a thing of beauty. In between my own chuckles, I nodded my head contentedly, relishing the satisfaction of God in seeing one of his kids released into his true calling. There is very likely much more to my friend's destiny than what I observed that evening, but watching him clown around while delivering a dead serious sermon elicited in me a deep cosmic happiness.

I expect that most of us have touched the hem of our destiny in similar fashion. Some endeavor makes us feel fully alive on the inside, and we know that we're moving closer to our real purpose. Our hearts soar, and we are all there as we soak up the thrill of knowing God is working through our lives—and working well—as we wait. Something is happening that makes us feel as if we're beginning to be what God has always meant us to be. What greater thrill is there?

The Promise of Destiny

Think about this: destiny is good because God is good.

Dare we believe either? Dare we feel the primal stirring of unacknowledged destiny? Can we even consider that the purpose of God for our lives may be much grander and deeper and harder and more wonderful than we have admitted to our closest friends ...or even to ourselves? If that possibility excites you even while it disturbs you, then keep reading. In the chapters that follow, we will journey into this new realm. The realm of possibility. The realm of purpose. And make some sense of the process involved in obtaining our destiny.

What we now see are but the first steps in the progression toward purpose—the first stages in the epic drama of God's redemptive wildness loosed on earth. If this be so, it changes everything! The mere thought of it expands the scope of our lives exponentially. If it's true, then passages of scripture that used to be mere rhetoric suddenly burst upon us with opportunity and challenge. Words like "Whoever wants to save his life will lose it, but whoever loses his life for me will find it" (Matthew 16:25). Verses like "You are not your own; you were bought at a price. Therefore honor God with your body" (1 Corinthians 6:19–20). Or this one: "I tell you the truth, anyone who has faith in me will do what I have been doing. He will do even greater things than these, because I am going to the Father" (John 14:12). And then there's a well-known verse few of us know what to do with: "Blessed are the meek, for they will inherit the earth" (Matthew 5:5). My own loose translation of that mysterious verse goes like this: "Let go of the smallness of your own pursuits, and join me in the bigness of my Kingdom; our destiny, you and me together, is to bring the very essence of heaven to earth!"

With God cooking up such amazing, miraculous, world-changing potential in our lives, why would he wait? Many times I don't get it. But we will.

I realize that all this glorious talk may seem far removed from the messy and mundane demands of your daily experience. Truth be told, I find that many Christians shrink from an honest appraisal of both ends of the spectrum: the pain and hardness of life as well as the glory and hope of our calling. It's easier (and less emotionally threatening) to narrow our expectation of life down to the mindless, single-syllable response given to most casual inquiries: "Fine."

"I'm fine." "Things are going fine." "The kids are fine." "Work's fine." And church? "Yeah, church is fine."

Okay, so sometimes we do find ourselves in the domain of fine—things aren't great, and they're not terrible. Life is just okay. But the trouble comes when fine gets too comfortable and we don't want to leave. We choose the perceived safety of fine over the honest tally of our life: "Much of the time my life feels simply hard and broken, but occasionally God brings me into moments of incomprehensible transcendence and is preparing me, I know, for things too wonderful even to give words to."

But I admit that when Kellie and I began setting up our new life in Greensboro, fine was a pretty fair assessment of where we were. I frequently found myself in the place of feeling *emotionally skinny.* Unwilling to verbalize my frustrations with God and sometimes unwilling to take my dreams out of their box and gaze at them again. It was easier to truncate the parts that lay furthest from my control: the extreme bad and extreme good. Fine would do fine.

But the willingness to be brutally honest about our current condition is the very quality that legitimizes our grandest dreams.

As Kellie and I left our friends at the beach, we struggled to wrap words around our conflicting emotions. Sometimes the dream was compelling—exciting us even as we continued to wait.

At other times we lost heart. But ultimately we were committed to walk the road before us, so we reached again for the grace to wait well.

WAITING WELL: HANNAH PURSUES A DESTINY

Hannah's dream was to have a son—not so remarkable as dreams go. But as ordinary as it was, it remained unfulfilled (see 1 Samuel 1:1–2:21). And as she longed for her stomach to grow, the only thing that grew was a gnawing emptiness...an emptiness that became a raging hunger inside her. And on the outside she endured the daily taunts and snubs of the "other woman" in her husband's life. Elkanah had two wives, which unfortunately was not uncommon in ancient Israel, and Peninnah had child after child while Hannah had none.

Her grief and shame overflowed her soul until one day she entered the house of the Lord and collapsed in tearful entreaty, wordlessly mouthing her heart's cry to God. Despairing, yet at the same time unwilling to let go of her hope, she held her destiny before the Father once again. I can almost hear her anguish: "Lord, you know I was created for more than this! Satisfy the ache inside me, and fulfill your calling on my life. Don't let the seasons pass me by and leave me desolate! Make good on the hope you have placed within me. Give me a son! He will belong to you all his days" (see 1 Samuel 1:10–11).

Who knows how many years Hannah had laid such a petition

at God's feet while she waited and prayed. Prayed and waited. Perhaps after five or six years her hope grew faint and she even stopped praying. But the dream didn't die. Maybe it emerged a couple of years later with fresh resolve or desperation and drove her to the house of the Lord on the day that Eli the priest observed her travail. The birthing of the dream in her soul was more exhausting than the birth from her body, which came in eventual answer to her waiting. The right dream, rightly held, will always be rightly fulfilled, even if the wait is long and hard.

Surely Hannah must have wondered, *Am I a fool to keep hoping and waiting and looking? Maybe I should just accept life on its own terms and forget this foolish vision.* Instead, she nourished her hope and stewarded her vision until God answered. And the result of her determination to hope and wait was not only her own redemption as a mother and wife but also the redemption of a nation in sore need of a godly leader. This seemingly ordinary desire—a woman longing to have a son—was in fact a destiny so large it's hard to fathom even in hindsight.

Hannah's son, Samuel, served God wholeheartedly from the time he was a small boy in the Temple until he was a very old prophet. He lived for God both while he served Eli the priest and while he served as God's mouthpiece during a time in Israel's history when the people weren't much for listening. Eventually he set the stage for Israel's greatest leader, King David, to replace one of its poorest leaders.

God used Hannah's years of hope and tears to deliver the baby who would grow up to be one of Israel's most important prophets. As wonderful as our dreams appear to us, we don't usually see the larger picture of how the fulfillment of our destiny intertwines with the destiny of many others. None of us lives in a vacuum. Our callings affect hundreds and even thousands of other lives—for good or ill—depending largely upon our willingness to endure the weakness of waiting, to go the distance, and to obtain our God-given future!

Strategic Scribblings

Journaling Strategy No. 1: Embrace the now.

Are you fighting the season of life that seems to have you mired in waiting? Or are you uncovering God's purpose during this season? Journal your engagement with this divine strategy of embracing the now.

_____

_____

_____

_____

_____

_____

_____

_____

_____

_____

_____

_____

_____

_____

_____

_____

_____

Chapter Two

Of Giants and Grasshoppers

Savoring the Winds of God's Favor

> Then Caleb silenced the people before Moses
> and said, "We should go up and take possession
> of the land, for we can certainly do it."
> But the men who had gone up with him said,
> "We can't attack those people; they are stronger
> than we are.… All the people we saw there
> are of great size.… We seemed like grasshoppers
> in our own eyes, and we looked the same to them."
> —NUMBERS 13:30–33

I couldn't suppress a dazed grin as I put down the telephone and turned to Kellie. "You're not going to believe this, but it looks like we have an answer to our prayers!"

When we had arrived in Greensboro two months earlier, we were graciously invited by Kellie's parents to live in their home while we looked for one of our own. After several weeks they left to spend the next four months outside the country. It was a tremendous blessing to have our own place, even though we were living out of suitcases while most of our things remained in storage. We launched out expectantly to house hunt, looking for land with the hope of building a house.

But as summer waned, so did our hopes. It was a classic situation to be sure: everything we liked was too expensive, and what we could afford was less than exciting. We had a clear and somewhat idyllic picture of what we wanted. It sat on the outskirts of town on a large private lot with room for the kids to play and for us to garden. Plus a creek would be nice. It would be a country French house where we would live happily ever after.

After a while it appeared we might have to ratchet that dream down a few notches.

Even though we had moved to Colorado two years earlier without having a place to live and knowing scarcely a soul, we had gotten pretty comfortable with our life there. Now, back in North Carolina, we had to face again the intimidating task of finding a place for ourselves. And once again we were looking for a home without the stabilizing effect of having a real job.

After looking at a hundred possibilities and saying no a hundred times, we saw our bank balance dwindle dangerously close to nothing. Then it wasn't quite so much fun anymore. Where once we'd been energized by the towering quest before us, we began to feel like grasshoppers dodging the feet of giants! We had to confront the daunting challenge: would we fight for a dream or run away from the risk? Well, we might become grasshopper road kill, but for the present we'd go after the giant.

So much for pluck and blind faith. Two months later we still had nothing to show for our house search. And worse, our dream of launching oneFlesh Ministries began to look like a receding glimmer. Even if we did find just the right house, there was still the small matter of paying for it. Paying for anything, really. The equity from our last house was used to fund our Colorado Sabbatical; how would we pull off buying a place now?

That's when the phone rang, and I'm not speaking metaphorically. I was startled to hear my uncle's voice on the other end. I hadn't spoken with him for several years, but he just happened to want to invest in the family business that my grandfather had begun, of which I had part ownership. Would I be interested in selling part of my share, he wondered. Well, as a matter of fact, yes! If we could find a house we liked, we now had a decent down payment. *God, you are truly amazing!*

The elation of that divine rescue of our struggling dream lingered for months as we reveled in the wonder of God's eleventh-hour breakthroughs. This was the second time that God had intervened, without natural explanation, to pull us back from a financial precipice and secure our course. The first time had come a year and a half before, when we felt the threat of a financial free fall in Colorado. Out of nowhere, a real-estate agent mailed every home in our old North Carolina neighborhood (where we still owned a home), saying she had a family determined to live in that community. Within a couple of weeks and without even putting our house on the market, we had a full-price offer that covered all our debts and gave us a tidy sum to live on for the remaining year in Colorado Springs.

Wow. Was it more awe or relief that we felt? Whatever it was, it brought us to our knees in worship. God's kindness and favor to us were becoming a new and deeper part of our understanding. No longer was God good in a vague, theoretical sense. Now he was good *to us!* The fundamental goodness of his essence broke in upon us, and we saw that he can be nothing other than good. This began a deep awakening: daring to believe that we actually live underneath the favor of God.

I don't think I'm that different from you, because we both live in a culture driven by performance. We work harder and harder to earn a commendation, a raise in pay, a promotion, or new opportunities. With so much of our earthly life geared to earning the favor of people, it's tough to absorb a favor that supercedes our tarnished efforts. The grace in which we stand is the eternal exhibit of Isaiah 55:9—"As the heavens are higher than the earth, so are my ways higher than your ways and my thoughts than your thoughts"!

WINDS OF GOD'S FAVOR

Because the heart of God is goodness itself, he is determined to show kindness toward the work of his hands, indiscriminately.

Therefore, "he causes his sun to rise on the evil and the good, and sends rain on the righteous and the unrighteous" (Matthew 5:45). This is the first of three levels of blessing, and it's known as common grace. It's the goodness of God lavished upon the world without regard for who we are, what we believe, or what we do.

The second level of blessing flows out of the law of sowing and reaping. God has determined that there is an automatic consequence to every action, every word, every thought, every intention of the heart. Through this dynamic we reap blessings in our lives by righteous behavior...whether intentional or not. We all reap what we sow, both in this world and for the next. This is simply another opportunity for God to pour his loving-kindness into our lives because, just as a harvest exceeds what was sown, so God returns much greater blessing to us than what we planted. Even here, God's system is not the cold machinery of justice. Far from that, this legal system is infused with grace and mercy.

But the third level of blessing is where God's utter delight in his powerful goodness shines brightest. Here, in the lives of his children, God actually causes *everything*—absolutely all things without exception—"to work together for good to those who love God" (Romans 8:28, NASB). This is mind-boggling! God, who is able to do any good thing he wants, has decided to do *every* good thing toward his sons and daughters. In miraculous fashion he looks for opportunity after opportunity to shine favor upon his children. And not only that, he takes every hellish volley of pain and suffering (of which the world is full) and redemptively transforms it from death to life.

This is the God we have as Father. And this is the Father who leads us tenderly and purposefully into seasons of waiting.

And so the man or woman who lives in the present awareness of heaven's favor lives in a part of heaven itself and, to that extent, brings heaven to earth. We fulfill the prayer of Jesus that resonates across all time: let your Kingdom come! (see Matthew 6:10). And so that Kingdom does come...*especially as we wait.* Waiting is loaded with redemptive promise.

CAMPERS AND HIKERS

Waiting isn't easy, no matter how you approach it. But neither is it optional, so we are left to choose only *how* we will wait: it can be either actively or passively.

I think the world can be divided into two sets of people: campers and hikers. Since I like to do both, I don't mean to disparage either group. But by way of illustration, campers are the ones who prefer to play it safe. They find a quiet, livable spot, set up camp, and remain within the boundaries of what is known and familiar. They don't reach to learn or grow; all they seek is to make themselves as comfortable as possible and enjoy the view.

In contrast, hikers stay on the move. Not content to live small lives, they have to see what's around the next switchback in the trail and enjoy the view from the top of the peak. They push beyond the boundaries of what is known in search of what is new. Willing to take the risk of confronting uncertain challenges and even dangers, they press forward in discovery. As a result, they constantly have to adapt and learn…to stretch, to fail, and to grow. This is the kind of person I want to be.

But it's not always the person I am! Sometimes I choose the attraction of comfort and security and revert to being a camper. Sometimes safety feels too precious to gamble on new pursuits. Sometimes I choose a small world…and suffer the loss of precious opportunities in God.

There's some camper and some hiker in each of us, though one will usually shove its way to the fore. When it comes to waiting, we have to choose between hunkering down in self-protection or running the risk to reach for God in the midst of adversity. When Israel faced the challenge of occupying their Promised Land, it was no accident that the defenders were huge. And it's not by mistake that the table of provision God spreads for us with such abundance lies smack in the middle of enemies, as Psalm 23 reminds us. Still, the feast is real, and it's served up for grasshoppers like us.

PLACES WE CAN'T GO

There are simply things we can't learn and places we can't go without hiking through land controlled by giants. Everyone gets a turn against the big boys; it's just a matter of time. My friends Kim and Kathy Wenzel had to cross the terrain of giants recently when they stepped out to launch a ministry to burned-out ministers. Kathy was reflecting on Jesus' boat ride through the storm (Luke 8:22–25):

I am coming to understand a little more about "Be still and know that I am God" in our own difficult, sometimes desperate situations. Do you ever feel that life is really a great big roller coaster, sometimes straight and fast, sometimes upside down and frightening, sometimes coming to a painful and sudden stop?

Is there something in this Christian experience that is supposed to be thrilling, challenging, and fear-expelling? Forcing us to face our fears is really a big part of what Jesus is doing in us. Are we afraid of poverty? He may make us face it. Are we afraid of losing our position? That may happen. Are we afraid of becoming a nobody with no friends, no one to respect us? This, too, could happen. Yet, Jesus is right there beside us, going through the whole experience with us.

Maybe if we just expect to be challenged on all our fears, we can see our way to the end of the ride and feel the rush of having finished it, in one piece, with a whole lot more faith under our belts. Expect life to throw you a lot of curves. You are in training today to become a ruler in eternity. Don't worry about the people who seem to be gliding through life. They just haven't had their turn yet![1]

We each get a turn on the roller coaster. And part of the process of waiting is learning not to fear that experience but instead to see the kindness of God drawing us to himself in a brand-new way. Toward a whole new depth of intimacy and maturity and wisdom. We are learning to be trail-savvy hikers!

The Oasis

Kellie and I only vaguely realized we were grasshoppers entering the land of giants. Graciously, God sent us a haven for our souls, and that was a church family.

We visited several places that had been recommended by friends, but none felt like home. Venturing farther afield, we visited a church that had hosted a conference we'd attended many years before. Since I am fascinated by models and approaches to "doing church," I usually spend the first visit scoping out everything the congregation and leadership do, from printed pieces to programming to P.A. equipment to pulpit personalities. Everything that announces: "This is who we are. This is what we do and why."

I was definitely in this mode upon entering what was to become our home church, but as the first note of worship sounded, I was carried away. Instead of studying their techniques and technology, I was caught up in a nearness of Jesus that seemed so tangible I could have touched him. The music faded quickly into the background, and I was overcome by the Presence, held captive for about forty-five minutes. I couldn't (or wouldn't) open my eyes. I just wanted to be still, to soak in the warmth of heaven. Kellie and I waited until we were eating lunch to ask each other the "Well, what did you think?" question, but it was merely a formality. We knew already, even though we didn't know a soul in this church, that we'd come home.

The music wasn't fancy and the facility wasn't lavish, but if God was there, that was enough for us. That weekly drink of God was going to be an oasis for us in the months of desert to come. Even in the most barren places, God opens up little wells of refreshment to keep our soul and our soul's dream alive.

Why does he bother? Because he is good. To you and to me.

THE RUB

The goodness of God, it seems to me, is the central issue of life. It is also the central issue for us to remember when waiting for destiny to become reality. Is God *really* good when I am waiting? And waiting? And waiting some more? Waiting chafes on our soul the way a new hiking boot raises a blister on our heel. Something feels so wrong, but here again God draws us below the surface of discomfort into a deeper understanding of purpose.

Strategy No. 2: *Allow the rub of waiting to confirm your larger destiny.*

This friction, the rub that at first irritates, leads to our second strategy for navigating divine delays gracefully: allow the rub of waiting to confirm your larger destiny. In other words, the very frustration you feel at the smallness of your current world is proof positive that you were, in fact, made for more! It is the imprint of God's purpose on your life that causes you to chafe during the season of preparation. If you weren't made for more, you'd be happy in your limited sphere, but God has given you a destiny, and you won't be content until you fully possess that calling. Can you receive that hope in your soul?

THE GROAN

Waiting is a confusing process. Being given a purpose by God seems inevitably to involve pain. And when faced with pain, we reflexively pull back.

Consider the passage I quoted earlier: "We know that in all things God works for the good of those who love him, who have been called according to his purpose" (Romans 8:28). That verse can be the wellspring of hope...and it can also be the bane of soul-sick bitterness when we can't see even a ray of goodness in some of the "all things" we're facing.

But this verse begins to take on a world of import when we zoom out to the larger view of chapter 8. Beginning in verse 17, Paul unpacks the purpose we are made for with an unwelcome caveat: the glory God wants to give us as his sons and daughters (our inheritance as children) requires that we experience a certain measure of suffering. *Okay, Paul, this is beginning to sound like the opposite of good news, but go on.*

Paul hurries to add, "I consider that our present sufferings are not worth comparing with the glory that will be revealed in us" (Romans 8:18). *So...the stab of the dentist's needle does hurt, but the*

Novocain then allows him to redeem the decay and restore the glory of a happy smile.

Paul then uses a childbirth metaphor. The entire world is groaning as the pains of labor ricochet across its body. But it's a pain with purpose! A new life is coming—a never-been-seen-before revelation of who we really are. Children of God! Liberated. Redeemed. Glorious.

What could that mean? Whatever it does mean stretches our mental capacity. We're all too familiar with the dirt and slime of our lives, so we forget that underneath the beggar's rags we are more glorious than angels. In this world we are growing in glory every time we represent the beauty of heaven with a redemptive word or a compassionate smile or a prayer of faith or a pure heart.

Can you see it? That's why we groan!

Our groaning is simultaneously an agonizing cry of distress with what we sometimes are…as well as a deep-hearted petition for what we are becoming…as well as an unspeakable expression of adoration to the God of glory who is our Father! We groan with discomfort, we groan with yearning, and we groan because we can't always express our love to God in words.

These groans are an unceasing intercession that wordlessly rises to heaven out of the fabric of our being. And occasionally we tap into this spiritual river of worship with our words of intercessory prayer. This intercession is the *intersection* between a profound contentment in God and a wrenching discontent with the lack of God's glory in our earthly lives.

We are made for glory. This is transforming truth, not a trite religious expression. It represents the wonder of God in his transcendence as well as his intention to transcend our fallenness with his beauty. But I had never dared to apply this truth to my own life.

Somehow the nature of God-ness is demonstrated in the infinite replication of his glory throughout creation. This is the drama we live within, and we are all players, as Shakespeare well noted, upon the stage of a glorious story. It is *the* Story, in fact, and our part to play is fairer—yes, more glorious—than we dare believe.

> The created world itself can hardly wait for what's coming next. Everything in creation is being more or less held back. God reins it in until both creation and all the creatures are ready and can be released at the same moment into the glorious times ahead. Meanwhile, the joyful anticipation deepens. (Romans 8:19–21, MSG)

As Kellie and I waited restlessly, the phone call from my uncle broke across our groaning with a ray of glory. It resuscitated our expiring vision! *We can do this,* we suddenly felt. *We will find a house, and the requests for us to extend our oneFlesh ministry will start coming in. The impossible dream really is happening!*

Of all the pieces of this dream, the house was the most tangible, and so the house became more than just a practical need to be met. It became symbolic of our future, symbolic of God's call on our lives. Maybe the grasshoppers do win in the end.

Waiting Well: Joshua and Caleb Know Where to Look

These two men are honored in Scripture for their vision and commitment to God's destiny in their lives and in the life of the nation of Israel. Numbers 13–14 tells us the end of their story—and it's a glorious ending. But these two men were remarkable because of the faith and confidence they displayed in the *middle* of the story. Along with the millions of Hebrews that Moses led out of Egypt, Joshua and Caleb saw the miraculous provision and protection of God time after time. And when they stood on the edge of Canaan—at the border of their destiny—their hearts surely beat with anticipation. But after their forty-day spy tour of the Promised Land, along with ten other Hebrew spies, their passion was irrepressible!

No amount of giants and fortresses could deter them from God's promise. They saw the land, they tasted its fruit, and then—through no fault of their own—they were subjected to a very long waiting season. Not months, not a year or two, but forty years of desert duty before they were allowed even to begin to receive their inheritance. The one thing that must have sustained them was knowing where to focus—not on the giants but on their God!

Now contrast these men who waited well with the larger number who did not trust God's promises. Ten leaders of God's people —eyewitnesses to the ten plagues back in Egypt, who walked through the Red Sea on dry ground, who watched the cloud of glory and pillar of fire appear every day and every night to guide them through the wilderness—said, "No! God can't do it for us.

The promise is too grandiose and the obstacles too enormous. It won't happen."

The lesson from Joshua and Caleb is to move when God is moving, wait when God is waiting, and trust that every word of promise spoken by our heavenly Father will come to pass in perfect time. The giants will fall eventually. Facing what must have felt like overwhelmingly bitter disappointment, these two guys remained confident that they would live to see their faith rewarded. And guess what? They were rewarded!

Listen to the testimony of these courageous souls forty-five years later as they stood, once again, upon the edge of Canaan's promise. Caleb speaks to Joshua...

> You know what the LORD said to Moses the man of
> God at Kadesh Barnea about you and me. I was forty
> years old when Moses the servant of the LORD sent me
> from Kadesh Barnea to explore the land. And I brought
> him back a report according to my convictions, but my
> brothers who went up with me made the hearts of the
> people melt with fear. I, however, followed the LORD
> my God wholeheartedly. So on that day Moses swore
> to me, "The land on which your feet have walked will
> be your inheritance and that of your children forever,
> because you have followed the LORD my God whole-
> heartedly."
>
> Now then, just as the LORD promised, he has kept me
> alive for forty-five years since the time he said this to Moses,

while Israel moved about in the desert. So here I am today, eighty-five years old! *I am still as strong today as the day Moses sent me out; I'm just as vigorous to go out to battle now as I was then.* Now give me this hill country that the LORD promised me that day. You yourself heard then that the Anakites were there and their cities were large and fortified, but, the LORD helping me, I will drive them out just as he said. (Joshua 14:6–12)

Does that give you goose bumps as it does me? After forty-five years of waiting, Caleb's strength of heart and body was as potent as ever as he strained to get his hands on the giants of the hill country—the same giants who frightened the other spies so long ago. Our destiny, like Caleb's, is to be giant-killing grasshoppers!

Strategic Scribblings

Journaling Strategy No. 2:
Allow the rub of waiting to confirm your larger destiny.

Are you gripped by a sense of destiny or an overarching vision that God has given for your life (whether large or small)? What commitment are you willing to make now to see that vision fulfilled? What will your commitment mean in terms of time, money, prayer, and waiting? Write down your thoughts.

Chapter Three

Flying on Instruments

A Voice in the Fog

> Rarely do significant shifts come without a
> sense of our being lost in dark woods…that
> place in life where you know all the words
> but none of the music.
> —SUE MONK KIDD[1]

I was up in the Blue Ridge Mountains a couple of months ago for one of my three-day writing retreats. This little mountain town where my family has vacationed since I was a boy is one of my favorite spots in the world. In the late seventies my grandfather Hugh built a little house that he used for a summer home, which meant it was up for grabs in the winter. So this simple, cozy house with the stone fireplace became my family's Christmas destination of choice.

So it is with a longstanding affection that I come up here now with my children…or, in the case of writing retreats, alone. I had packed my extensive wardrobe of jeans and sweatshirts, along with a bag of mysteriously fragrant dummy-proof meals from Kellie, and headed up to the high air and amazing vistas of…fog. Yes, fog is a staple of mountain life in the East, and truth is, I like it. At least for brief periods. While I'm really more of a sunshine hound, there is a magical, mystical fantasia as fog rolls in with gray, wispy bundles—sifting in and out of the sturdy, ancient conifers—until the gray blanket is pulled up over my eyes, and I can't see the house next door.

This time, as the fog hung close for two days, cabin fever struck, and I launched out for an early morning walk. I could see twenty to thirty feet in front of me, enough visibility to follow the path on its mile-long circuit through woods and meadow. It was an eerie yet enticing atmosphere that conjured adventuresome images as I zipped my fleece pullover up to my neck.

As I walked, I began to realize that I was relying heavily upon my sense of hearing to observe what was going on around me. *Funny,* I thought, *how much we rely on our vision when we can see, but then how automatically we begin to listen more intently when we can't see.* As I noticed this, I began to listen more intentionally to all the sounds around me.

When I arrived back at the house, I grabbed pen and paper to make a list of the auditory clues that hinted at the unseen things that had been going on around me. The crows cawing obnoxiously, the wind whistling quietly along the ridges, some hammers falling in the distance as work progressed on a new house, an occasional car creeping cautiously through the mist. I knew all these activities were taking place around me because I could hear them, and that was enough.

I dropped my pen and, rocking slowly in the weathered deck chair, began to sense a deeper significance to this experience. Fog, huh? Not unlike this season of waiting. I can see far enough ahead to keep walking but not enough to know what lies ahead or on either side. As I write this, I can't envision much of what lies beyond two or three months ahead. The bigger picture of my life is cloaked in an impenetrable gray.

Here on the mountain I can't see, but I can hear. What's the spiritual translation of that? A friend recently gave me a book called *Sacred Pathways*. The thesis of this insightful volume is that spirituality is not a one-size-fits-all affair. God speaks to one person most clearly out in a wooded sanctuary; to another, God reveals himself through ancient symbols and liturgy. Still another finds the voice of God echoing through the cinder-block room of a homeless shelter as she offers a blanket and sandwich.[2]

The author lets us know we don't have to conform to the narrow standards of others, nor are we to force on our friends the things that bring life to us. But the book hints at something beyond this—that we can enlarge our experience of God by discovering new pathways in our spiritual journey. This conviction breathes new purpose into our times of waiting.

Waiting seasons almost always incorporate a thick fog that rolls in to obscure our established channels of communication with the Father. Suddenly, overnight even, the timeworn passage we have walked in our relationship with Christ appears sealed off. Twinges of panic tug at the corners of our soul as we seek to steady ourselves. That which has anchored us, secured us, and imparted meaning seems to have vanished in the mist. And a deep cry issues forth from our soul: "My God, my God, why have you forsaken me?"

But...wait. As our hands grope blindly in the dark fog, we begin to hear something...some One actually...calling, comforting, speaking, loving us. And leading us through the fog into destiny.

REDEMPTION

One thing God wants to sow into the deepest channels of our soul is that there truly is no way we can lose with him. Though we would never seek out suffering, this world has plenty, and followers of Jesus will experience it. But there is no pain or difficulty that God does not fully redeem.

I do not wish to downplay the suffering that we endure in this world. On the battleground of planet Earth, the horrors of war surround us both physically and spiritually. In contrast to my rather sheltered life, untold numbers suffer atrocities beyond mention and beyond understanding. Pain is real. And pain is precisely the venue where men and women begin to live out their eternal citizenship in the here and now. Pain without redemption mocks our powerlessness with the taunts of hell. But in the starkest of contrasts, pain that is irresistibly transformed by redemptive kindness is the very incense of heaven on the earth. Both are a down payment of Kingdom realities to come.

Redemption is the essence of the gospel. And Jesus is the chief expression of God's redemptive intent. Satan will never ever stand a chance before him because there is no killing, stealing, or destroying that God can't replace, renew, and redeem (see John 10:10). Whether we recognize it or not, this redemptive aspect of God's nature is always in play. It is absolutely central to his character.

What we think of as salvation is not the end of redemption; it is the beginning of a life of constant, unending redemption. Every loss, every place of pain is destined to become a Tent of Meeting—holy ground where God encounters us, heals us, and gives us more than we lost. Only God could take our losses and cause them to be sources of strength, life, and renewal. This is heavenly in the truest sense. This is what we are made for!

Sometime ago it struck me that just about every serious movie I've seen follows the story line of redemption. The story unfolds by illuminating something that is broken. A situation is broken, people are broken, relationships are broken, dreams are broken…or perhaps just out of reach. Characters enter the story. Some are noble, some aren't. Conflict arrives in the form of a villain. But a thread of hope runs throughout that there just might be a possibility for redemption. And by the end of the story, almost always some form of redemption has taken place. Even in the grittier movie genres, redemption seems to finally appear. It may take a different form than the viewer originally expects, but it comes nevertheless.

Why would this be? If we assume that many leading film-makers have not experienced spiritual redemption, why does the theme of redemption still dominate the essence of story? Because, whether we recognize it or not, we all live within the Redemptive Story. The heartbeat of human existence is paradise lost and paradise redeemed! We crave it; we can't help looking for it; we are made for it.

And our times of waiting—as painful as they are—deliver one of life's most redemptive opportunities. When our normal connection to God is obstructed, we can carve out new channels of connection and life. The end result is that we are enriched, not impoverished! God's river of life is always flowing to us; we just have to learn how to find it in new places and drink.

Strategy No. 3:
Search out new paths of communion with God.

When God sends a fog, we learn to listen more intentionally. We find multiple new ways of drawing upon and receiving from him. Then when the fog lifts, we find that we have that much more access to him. In the fog we might learn to meet him in the quietness of contemplation; perhaps the awakened sense is the fellowship of dance and celebration. The new pathway for you might be a rediscovered love for the Scriptures and a whole new experience of knowing and loving God through those ancient words. The point is that we are learning not to languish in waiting but to find

and harvest its unique opportunities. And the attenda[...]
to actively search out new paths of communion with C[...]
special times.

✳ THE BLESSING OF TESTING ✳

It is crucial to know that we are not tested by waiting because God is unhappy with us. In fact, it is quite the opposite. It is those who please God—those who faithfully seek God and live for him— who receive the blessing of testing.[3] *Well, that's one blessing I could do without,* you might be thinking. But is it? I'm not so sure.

Hezekiah was king of Judah in the time of the prophet Isaiah. Stemming the tide from the reign of his wicked father, King Ahaz, Hezekiah quickly restored the nation to the worship of God. He humbled himself and led the people in a vast demonstration of repentance from the sins of their fathers and reinstituted the cele-bration of the Passover. "There was great joy in Jerusalem," we read, "for since the days of Solomon son of David king of Israel there had been nothing like this in Jerusalem" (2 Chronicles 30:26).

You'd think Hezekiah would be nominated for the Nobel prize. But instead, God rewarded Hezekiah by sending Sen-nacherib, king of Assyria, to pay a visit. With tremendous courage, Hezekiah restored the walls and defenses of Jerusalem in defiance of this foe, encouraging the people that God would deliver them against an incredibly powerful enemy. As Sennacherib laid siege to the city, he launched a massive propaganda initiative to dishearten the city, ridiculing their God, their king, and their people. Things did not look good for Hezekiah. *Will you really come through and deliver us, God?* he must have wondered.

Why reward a righteous king with an enemy siege? Because God tests those he loves. It's part of his wise process for purifying us. It reveals what is in us and what needs our attention. James says, "Blessed is the man who perseveres under trial, because when he has stood the test, he will receive the crown of life that God has promised to those who love him" (1:12). Hezekiah passed the test, and the Lord rewarded him by sending an angel to annihilate the Assyrian army! Not bad. Further, God made Hezekiah one of the richest kings in Israel's history.

So was the testing over? Nope. Years later Hezekiah became ill to the point of death. The prophet Isaiah even confirmed that Hezekiah would indeed die. But Hezekiah cried out to the Lord, and before Isaiah even left the palace, God said that he would extend the king's life by fifteen years. As if that weren't enough, God brought a miraculous sign to confirm the healing: the sun's shadow would back up ten steps on the king's stairway.

Was the testing over now? Not yet. Babylonian envoys were sent to Hezekiah sometime later to inquire about this amazing miracle. Then Scripture records that "God left him" right at that crucial moment. With pagans arriving in Jerusalem specifically to hear about the acts of the One True God, why would God suddenly hide? The reason: "to test him and to know everything that was in [Hezekiah's] heart" (2 Chronicles 32:31). Whatever this "leaving" of God looked like, it was surely disorienting and distressing in the extreme. But God's purpose was not for punishment; it was not even meant to produce patience. It was to reveal Hezekiah's heart. Not to God—he already knew! It was to reveal Hezekiah's heart to himself.

And this is the blessing of our times of waiting, the blessing God offers us when he seems to have disappeared. We get the chance to have our hearts filleted open for all to see.

Essentially, God sets a torch to the structure of our soul to see what it's made of. "If any man builds on this foundation using gold, silver, costly stones, wood, hay or straw, his work will be shown for what it is, because the Day will bring it to light. It will be revealed with fire, and the fire will test the quality of each man's work. If what he has built survives, he will receive his reward. If it is burned up, he will suffer loss" (1 Corinthians 3:12–15). To have the temporal stuff burned out of our heart is a blessing indeed… one of the great opportunities of waiting times.

Fog Causes Accidents

Despite all the beauty of fog and the potential blessings that come with it, fog also can create havoc. I remember a fog-filled Christmas at my grandfather's mountain house. I was a young teenager, and a heavy snow had knocked out the power in the neighborhood. *Awesome!* Now the adventure kicked into high gear! We had to heat the central room with the fireplace and use candles to see.

Having no stove or oven, we set out in search of an open restaurant. Afterward, as we drove back up the mountain to the house, the fog dropped in like a blanket, and we had only six feet of visibility in front of our snow-crusted headlights. Barely enough to distinguish the snow-colored road from the snow-colored drifts beside the road. We crested a hill, looking desperately for our left-hand turn off the main avenue. Dad thought he saw it and made the turn… Whoomp! As my brother and I piled out of the lodged car, we saw that we had turned about fifty feet too soon, plowing deeply into the wall of snow kicked up by the road plow.

My younger brother, Josh, and I tried valiantly to free the car but without success. We were stuck! Stuck and cold to boot. It couldn't get any worse. Or maybe it could. About that time a car came around the bend from the opposite side of the hill. It wasn't going fast, but by the time the driver saw us and hit the brakes, it was coming right for us. The car skidded on ice for twenty or thirty feet before whacking the rear end of our car.

While Josh and I watched helplessly, my sister Nana got thrown around the backseat. We were okay, but Nana was pretty bruised, and it put a damper on our Christmas vacation to say the least. That particular "testing blessing" went to my dad, who had to fight though a fog of depression before finding the grace of giving thanks for God's mercies.

Years later I experienced my own foggy collision. Kellie and I were still in house-hunting mode as summer gave way to fall. We felt as though we were getting chewed up between the gears of our

Colorado idealism and the harsh realism we were encountering in North Carolina. The house plans we had fallen in love with a year earlier were now stuck away somewhere as we canvassed yet another neighborhood, looking for an existing house to buy.

There was one neighborhood in particular that wowed us from the beginning. Large, beautiful homes on spacious lots surrounded by white-fenced horse pastures. This postcard scene appeared to be a rural spread but was actually right in town. Perfect. Except for one glitch—we couldn't afford either of the two houses for sale there!

Well, maybe if we sold off a couple of kids we might afford the "cheap" one. Meantime, I vacillated between the idealism of "God wants to bless us; he will provide" and a more visceral sense of fatalism. As it turned out, on one of my upswings I convinced Kellie that we could buy the less expensive house. Our offer was accepted. Wow! This house was older and needed work, but it was humongous! A palace.

At some point during the parade of contractors marching through, leaving stunningly large estimates in their wake, I woke up. The dream had become a nightmare. I desperately crunched numbers late one night, calculating taxes and utility costs to heat and cool that massive structure. And I learned that the neighborhood's lovely horse pastures are maintained by stratospheric homeowners association fees. I panicked, wondering how I'd break this devastating news to Kellie. *Oh, God, how could you have let me get into this mess?* I cried. *Aren't you with us anymore?*

But he was still with us. And although I felt as if I were stuck in a snowbank watching the lights of oncoming traffic skid toward us, his deliverance came. And the test revealed some things in our hearts that needed his work. God's help didn't come without pain, but it did redeem my foolish decision. We found that a lot of that first year was about God's pulling out all the rugs from underneath us. He stripped away our dreams and hopes, our expectations and securities, just to see if we would cling to him and his promises over us. And by the skin of our teeth, we clung.

Numbly at times, we clung. When we were alienated from one another and our one-flesh banner mocked us, we still clung. We might not be able to find hope, but we would not embrace hopelessness. If it were all a lie and God's promises to us empty, then we would die holding on to the dream. And yes, it really did feel this nihilistic. Maybe it was something of what Hezekiah felt as he looked out over the city walls at a vast military machine ready to chew up Jerusalem and spit out the bones.

At the cost of two thousand dollars, some hurt feelings, deeply shaken hopes, and not a few tears, we were released from our contract to buy that great old house. It would be some months before we would be able to appreciate this particular test that left our dreams feeling violated and abused. But eventually we were able to see the kindness of God that tests…and then redeems.

Flying on Instruments

That redemption reminds me of flying an airplane on instruments. My father was an air force pilot during the Vietnam War and used to talk occasionally about the challenge of flying, not by sight, but by what your instruments tell you. What you feel in the air is not always reliable; disorientation is customary for pilots, which is why they have to learn to trust their machines. When they don't trust them, they tend to die.

The artificial horizon on the attitude indicator tells the pilot how the plane is oriented—whether he is banking to one side or level. The altimeter tells him how high he is, and the airspeed indicator tells him how fast he is moving. Together with his compass, these three electronic gismos can get him safely back on the ground even after a fierce battle and in the blindness of fog.

When the fog rolls into your life in the form of waiting, Jesus Christ has never been more committed to redeeming your circumstances. He has not abandoned you; you just have to learn how to fly on instruments. Every instrument is a new pathway to Jesus and a chance to listen to his heartbeat. When you can't see in the thick fog, you can more clearly hear his whisper—*I love you. I'm with you. Don't be afraid. Trust me…learn from me. If you do, life can be fun again, and you'll come out on the other side that much closer to me and my promises over your life!*

WAITING WELL: JOHN THE BAPTIST SURVIVES A PARADIGM SHIFT

A wild man in the rich tradition of the Old Testament prophets (see Luke 7:17–35). A rough camelhair loincloth and tunic, bound together with a belt of animal skin. A scrounger of wild food. Probably wild-haired and maybe even wild-eyed, John the Baptist knew his purpose as well as his destiny. And he went at it day after day, urging people to repent and be baptized. To give up their dishonesty and hypocrisy and embrace the faith of their fathers.

More than that, he knew he was called to be the herald who would prepare the way for the Real Deal, the Messiah. So it must have been with an unearthly, intoxicating rush that he lowered the head of Jesus the Christ into the waters of the Jordan River in baptism. That act began John's waiting season.

As John continued to be faithful to his call, he watched and waited with puzzlement for Jesus to fulfill the prophetic word from John's own mouth: "He [Jesus] will baptize you with the Holy Spirit and with fire. His winnowing fork is in his hand, and he will clear his threshing floor, gathering his wheat into the barn and burning up the chaff with unquenchable fire" (Matthew 3:11–12). The wild man John must have anticipated a revolution or a spiritual conflagration with Jesus the Warrior setting things right for those who spurned God.

Instead, John had to wait for the big ending as he watched a campaign of mercy unfold. Jesus astounded everyone with miraculous healings, food multiplied to feed crowds, and rich words concerning his Father's heart and Kingdom. "This must be the preamble," John might have muttered to himself. "It's certainly not judgment day!" But it wasn't the preamble. Jesus came as the Shepherd to gather the hurt and broken and to show them the Father. Justice and retribution would come later.

After months and months of observing the gentle Shepherd, John was confused. The paradigm had changed, and the pathway that had led John in the purposes of God for years was suddenly obscured by a tremendous fog of uncertainty. As his internal tension mounted, John *had* to know the answer, so he sent a few of his followers to get to the bottom of things:

> When the men [John's disciples] came to Jesus, they
> said, "John the Baptist sent us to you to ask, 'Are you the
> one who was to come, or should we expect someone
> else?'"…
>
> So he replied to the messengers, "Go back and report
> to John what you have seen and heard: The blind receive
> sight, the lame walk, those who have leprosy are cured,
> the deaf hear, the dead are raised, and the good news is
> preached to the poor. Blessed is the man who does not
> fall away on account of me." (Luke 7:20, 22–23)

John, the man who had baptized Jesus; John, the fiery prophet who was kin to the Messiah. He had been tested in the fog. But out of this fog a fresh voice cut through to his understanding: there is another avenue for the Kingdom of God. It's not just about judgment; God also makes himself known in kindness and mercy. This was a real hurdle for John to get over, but we have every reason to think that he did survive this shift and embrace the larger purposes of God. And so must we. Our experience of God is so narrow and limited that we need the fog to force us outside our old ruts into larger channels of grace. God uses seasons of waiting to enlarge our understanding of and communion with him. That is part of the blessing and reward of waiting.

Strategic Scribblings

Journaling Strategy No. 3:
Search out new paths of communion with God.

How are you learning to receive the love of God in brand-new ways in your season of waiting? What are the fresh, new channels God is opening up to you now for communication and fellowship with him?

_____

_____

_____

_____

_____

_____

Chapter Four

Dreams for Sale

Waiting for Intimacy in the Desert

> ✳ God has not called us to do what seems
> possible, reasonable, or normally
> attainable.... We're supposed to be doing
> what is impossible and outrageous.
> —GRAHAM COOKE[1]

I recently took up the sport of tae kwon do. Probably because I've watched *The Matrix* more times than I care to admit. I'm an impressive yellow belt (translation: major rookie!). My excuse for going is that I take my son, Thorpe, with me, and it provides good father-son time.

Truth is, I just get a kick out of it. (This calls for a Dave Barry "har.") Last Saturday, though, was actually the first time I got kicked. *This is going to be so cool,* I thought as I strapped on my padded chest protector for the first time. But the instructor, instead of directing us onto the sparring mats, lined us up in pairs and prepared us to walk the length of the gym, facing one another. My partner was instructed to land a kick on my torso with every step.

He's only a kid, I told myself. But the twelve-year-old in front of me was a kid with a black belt and had about twenty pounds on me. "I don't like kicking skinny people," he told me encouragingly. "They're too bony!" But that didn't keep him from landing his kicks squarely and convincingly upon my bony little chest. After doing this for the full length of the gym, the kid had to tell me to breathe again. I was surprised there was any air left. Padding or no, this was not fun.

There is a point here, and it's this rib that's sticking out. No, it's that I'm beginning to learn that my opponent's strikes are something to be avoided. But more than that, those blows are an opportunity. Not just an opportunity to get bruised, but an opportunity to strike back. If you ever get the chance to watch a real master of tae kwon do, say, in the Olympics, you'll see a fluidity to his or her movements. Every time the opponent attempts a kick or punch, he is opening the door and inviting a counterattack. So an expert, in contrast to me, will move so gracefully that his block and counterstrike become one sweeping movement. Not a bad analogy to use for seasons of waiting.

I want to be one of those people you can't keep down. No matter what life throws at me, I want to bounce back. I want to live in such a way that every obstacle is strangely transformed into a benefit. I want to emerge from struggle stronger, wiser, better. The corny phrase "bitter or better" is excruciatingly appropriate here.

Let's be real. Every one of us has any number of ready-made opportunities to become bitter, especially in the disorienting fog where everything is either hidden or seen only in dim outline. People let us down. Plans don't work out. Even friends seem to forget you. God himself seems unpredictable. You feel let down regularly, but the point is, you don't go down! You learn and respond. You parry and thrust. Your left arm snakes down in a low block while your right knee swivels across, whipping your foot around in a roundhouse to the enemy's gut!

Life is full of blows to your dreams. The promises of God that used to burst with muscular potential are now being used for kicking practice—for the full length of the gym—and you're finding it hard to breathe.

As much as you may not want to accept it, this is by design. There's no other way.

WAITING IS ABOUT INTIMACY

No other way for what? No other way to develop intimacy. And intimacy is what all of this is about. Believe it or not, waiting is about intimacy. God's greatest purpose in seasons of waiting is to draw you close to himself, to reveal the depth of his commitment to you, and to equip you for your destiny. You might think he has a strange way of showing his love, but maybe *we're* the strange ones. Maybe God has things squared away, and we're the ones who are mixed up. One thing is sure: God's ways are different from ours... different and *better,* once we understand them.

> Take a good look, friends, at who you were when you got called into this life. I don't see many of "the brightest and the best" among you, not many influential, not many from high-society families. Isn't it obvious that God deliberately chose men and women that the culture overlooks and exploits and abuses, chose these "nobodies" to expose the hollow pretensions of the "somebodies"? (1 Corinthians 1:26–28, MSG)

In his wisdom, God uses our desert experiences to draw us close to himself, and this is the awesome opportunity presented to us in any season of waiting.

A CHANGE OF PERSPECTIVE

I gained a bit of insight into this dynamic when Kellie and I attended a conference last summer. The speaker was talking about how the road from Jesus' baptism to his first miracle ran through the desert. Whoa! All of a sudden I had a visual image of where Kellie and I were in our own journey. Our two years in Colorado were nothing short of a baptism—a resurrection to a sense of calling and purpose and expectancy we had never before tasted! And it tasted good. There was certainly no desert in view.

When God spoke to us about returning to North Carolina, we were sure this was the launching pad into the dream he had awakened in us. So when the road curved and the vegetation started getting sparse and the ground was dry and sandy, we didn't want to believe it. *Lord, there must be some mistake! This isn't what you promised.* But honestly it was, because God had promised us himself first. Being a little slow, we took more than a year to recognize that our desert experience was a call to intimacy.

The conference speaker was a remarkable man named Graham Cooke, and in his book *The Nature of God* he communicates a vital truth: "Whenever we move into a new spiritual dimension of our calling and our ministry, we must take the time to upgrade our relationship with God."[2] It's presumptuous to receive a call from God into a higher level of ministry and then simply leap in, thinking we already have everything we need for the job. Far from it, Cooke admonishes. The upgraded call is a call to upgrade!

And so God gently leads us into the desert for the intimate purpose of stripping away the baggage that will be dead weight in the new assignment. He calls us to the desert, where he can add new resources of strength, wisdom, courage, and character. The desert isn't a punishment; it's a gift! Not a gift we would ordinarily seek, but one we come to value and maybe eventually…even choose.

I read recently about the POW who was the ranking officer among the prisoners being held at the infamous Hanoi Hilton during the Vietnam War. For eight years, Adm. Jim Stockdale endured tortures of his own while inspiring and equipping hundreds of other men to survive the nightmare. He developed several key systems of communication, intelligence, and pain management that allowed his troops to pull together and endure their environment of brutality.

When asked how he managed to do it, he replied, "I never lost faith in the end of the story. I never doubted not only that I would

Strategy No. 4:
Let adversity become the means of your success.

get out, but also that I would prevail in the end and turn the experience into the defining event of my life, which, in retrospect, I would not trade."[3] This is a sobering testament to the power of hope and perspective. It also reminds me of the tae kwon do strategy: let your adversity become the very means of your success.

Could the waiting season you are in, with all its biting fear and doubt, become the defining event of your life? Could it actually be the source of intimacy and character that catapults you into your destiny rather than your biggest obstacle to it? Your perspective is what will determine whether adversity serves your destiny or derails it.

Adversity has another defining power. I heard someone say that adversity introduces us to ourselves. Unlike any other situation we encounter, difficulty strips away the pretense so that our heart condition can be exposed…to us! It tends to bring out the best and the worst of who we are, and both of these unmaskings are a gift.

As the crud surfaces in our souls, we have a chance to recognize it and deal with it. The better parts of our character also rise to the top, allowing us to lean on them and, ultimately, to lean on God as we pursue our dreams through the desert.

House Dreams and Dream Houses

While Kellie and I were waiting, with our dreams hanging in the balance, we actually did buy a house. After all the trials of searching and being disappointed and searching some more, we finally moved into a new house early in 2003. To be frank, even though it was nicer than any home we'd owned before, it wasn't the home I had dreamed of.

About a month after our earlier "perfect house" fiasco—the house from hell that cost me two thousand dollars—I found the next perfect house. Well, not quite perfect. It needed some work, but the setting was gorgeous, the location ideal, and the house had tons of potential. And we could not buy it!

We tried…twice! The house was tied up in a convoluted foreclosure and had sat empty for more than a year. You'd think that a bank would be salivating over an opportunity to unload such a mess, but no. They were adamant that it must sell for full price, and we couldn't go that high. *God, you're killing me here! Are you just toying with us?* Ah, perspective.

So much about the desert comes back to perspective. I remember an exchange in the movie *Notting Hill,* a romance story between a famous actress and a very ordinary British bookseller. Discovered at his house by the paparazzi, she flies into a rage. He tries to interject a lighthearted note of temperance. "Wait a minute," he pleads with her. "This is crazy behavior. Can't we just laugh about all this? Seriously, in the huge sweep of things, this stuff doesn't matter.... All I'm asking for is a normal amount of perspective."

"You're right. Of course, you're right," she responds with saccharine sweetness. Then, blurting suddenly in his face, "It's just that I've dealt with this garbage for ten years; you've had it for ten minutes! Our *perspectives* [she practically spits] are very different."[4]

And time is like that: as time passes, it begins to amplify unresolved tensions. So much so that we easily wind up with crazy behavior and irrational anger.

Time was beginning to feel like our enemy. Kellie's parents, who had graciously offered us the use of their house, had returned at Thanksgiving after being out of the country for four months. And while they weren't pressuring us, seven people living in their three-bedroom home was starting to make a sardine can look attractive. In desperation we checked out a house we'd driven past numerous times. "Well, it's not in a dream setting," we agreed, "but it is a beautiful, comfortable home." We decided that if we could get it for a good price, we'd go for it. The builder snapped up our substantially low offer, and we had ourselves a house.

For the first time in three years, we had all our possessions under one roof. I wondered later if I had settled for a lesser dream. But, after all, the house wasn't the dream. The house was just a house. And although it had become symbolic of the dream, we embraced this house as God's provision while holding on to the real dream—the chance to make a life out of building intimacy among God's people. Our dream was what we still called in our braver moments oneFlesh Ministries.

CARVING OUT SPACE...AGAIN

Kellie was a woman on a mission and whipped the house into a home in a matter of weeks—pictures on the walls and everything. As life began finally to take on a more even rhythm, I felt the temptation to allow life to lead us on its own terms. Life will do that. It pulls us incessantly toward spiritual laziness, which eventually dulls the soul and accumulates emotional clutter in lieu of intimacy.

The counterfeit presented by normal life had a comforting quality that we found quite appealing, especially after our many months of displacement and uncertainty. But God wouldn't let us lean back and relax in the new comfort of stability. We became discontent with our shallowness and realized we needed some soulspace.

Because I devoted my first book to the matter of soulspace, I'll offer only a brief overview here. Soulspace is about ruthlessly simplifying the interior of our mind and emotions from the clutter of external activity and distraction. It's about making room for the few things that really matter—God and the cluster of vital people in our lives.

Our culture is relentless in its determination to speed up the pace of life and to increase the demands we live with. Seasons of waiting, with all their apparent inactivity, can still be hijacked by the whirl and frenzy of outer motion. And this is where we must take a stand; it's a battle we dare not lose. Since heaven calls us to live according to its culture of freedom, we must turn a deaf ear to this world's siren call, lest we scuttle our destiny on the shoals of shallowness. Even the church can wind up being an unwitting ally of this destructive clutter. My friend Fil Anderson observes in his book *Running on Empty,* "One of my most grave concerns is that the church has joined forces with the world in a conspiracy of noise, busyness, and hurry. The outcome is that we are distracted from a life of intimacy with God and each other."[5]

The thing that makes soulspace such an essential pursuit in the life of the believer is that it's a gateway virtue. You know the idea: various low-risk illicit drugs are dangerous, not so much for what they do to the body directly, but because they open the door of opportunity to higher-risk drug use. In a similar but much more constructive way, soulspace is a gateway practice because it opens the door of opportunity to so many things God wants to do and say in our lives. Fundamentally, space of soul is the gateway to intimacy with God.[6]

So Kellie and I went back to the basics we had carved out in Colorado: extended, unhurried times of fellowship with the Lord, protected blocks of time with one another to pray and interpret life together, intentional investment in our children, and cultivating some key friendships that seemed to bear the promising marks of community.

Two Tests

As Kellie and I began to renew our soulspace, we still sensed a deep soul weariness, feeling that while life had stabilized, our elusive destiny was dying in the desert. And this is where you, too, will face the biggest desert test: will you jettison your calling and the things God has carefully deposited in your heart? You will be tempted to do that very thing and settle into the routines of normal life. In fact, there are two key tests that you face in the desert: the test of settling and the test of sacrifice.

The first test arrives when you are most vulnerable. You become thirsty and weary, and your dreams begin to waver like a mirage. In your fatigue, you're tempted to second-guess God's promises. *Maybe that dream wasn't really from God after all,* you think. *Maybe I just created those images of God using me because I wanted it to be true. Who am I to think God has given me a special destiny? Maybe it's time just to settle for the ordinary life everyone else is leading... It's not so bad.*

It's like the Jedi mind trick in *Star Wars.* Our Enemy whispers, *Who do you think you are?* And we echo in our discouragement, *Who do I think I am?* The Enemy continues, *If God had such great plans for you, he wouldn't have led you into this barrenness!* And we dutifully parrot, *Yeah, if God had such great plans for me, there is no way he would have dragged me into this parched place.*

And so settling becomes a very attractive option. It's not that you're going to deny God; you're still a Christian. Why not take the pressure off and just get on with the business of living life? But deep inside there's the sound of a small, persistent cry: *NO! Don't let go of God's promise. Don't bail out on your true destiny!* And that battle will continue until you draw a line in the hot sand and say, "Enough! 'Though he slay me, yet will I hope in him'" (Job 13:15).

Then there is the second test, the test of sacrifice, which takes that commitment one step further. Are you willing to give those dreams into the hand of God? Are you willing for God to take them from you and own them? Are you willing to take the dreams you have nurtured and protected—perhaps for years—and offer them up to God, even if he might kill them?

Abraham faced both of these tests—that of settling and that of sacrificing.

Waiting Well: Abraham Lays His Dream on the Altar

You probably know Abraham's story as well as you know your own. Abraham lives in a pagan nation. He knows there's a God but has never had personal contact with him. And not only that, but God has been silent for hundreds of years. Into that void God shows up and tells this brave soul to leave his country and go to a new land. God promises that Abraham will father a great nation and that he will be blessed. Not a bad deal, but can he trust this God? To Abraham's credit, at age seventy-five he leaves a comfortable existence in Ur and obeys God's command to set out for parts unknown.

When he arrives in Canaan, God speaks again and confirms that Abraham's children will own this country.

Ten years pass without any movement on the promise, and Abraham is getting concerned. He's eighty-five years old now and still has no son. Things are not looking good. But God speaks again and enlarges the promise. Not only will Abraham have a son, not only will his tribe become a great nation, but his descendants will populate the earth in numbers greater than the stars in the heavens. This must have strained his credibility in a big way. But Abraham "believed the LORD, and he credited it to him as righteousness" (Genesis 15:6). If you ask me, this is the definition of outrageous faith.

So Abraham has faith, but he doesn't fare too well in the test of *settling*. His wife, Sarah, instigates a plan—and Abraham concurs—to fulfill the promise through their own effort. The plan calls for Abraham to take Sarah's servant girl and try to conceive the promised son. It's not a perfect plan, but they figure it's close enough for government work. Sort of like God's promise. I guess it will have to do. But of course God's destiny is bigger than that, and the resulting child, Ishmael, isn't it.

Another fourteen years pass *(this is a long time, in case you hadn't noticed!)*, and Abraham is now one year short of one hundred. His hope must be about as shriveled as his body. God has the audacity to appear yet again and up the ante. He presses Abraham to change his and his wife's names—they were originally Abram and Sarai—so that every time they call one another by name, they will be declaring their apparently ridiculous destiny to everyone within earshot. "Pardon me, but would you pass the salt, Mother of Many Nations (Sarah)?" And as if that weren't enough, God calls Abraham to circumcise all the males in his household—a painful and unforgettable scar that serves as a memorial to the promised destiny that is not one whit closer to being fulfilled now than it was decades earlier.

But now God says, *One year and it will be done!*

Trust God or doubt him? Abraham wavers...but then draws a line in the sand: *I may be a fool, but I'll continue to give myself to this dream.* He accepts God's new names for him (meaning "father of many") and for Sarah (literally "princess" but interpreted by Scripture to mean "mother of many nations"). Then Abraham gets out a sharp blade to circumcise all the men that same day! In so doing, Abraham passes the test and rejects the temptation of settling.

The test of sacrifice comes a handful of years later when Isaac—the son of promise who had finally arrived—is perhaps eight or ten. God tells Abraham to take Isaac and actually sacrifice him on an altar. *What? I waited twenty-five years to see this promise fulfilled in my son, and now you want me to kill him? What kind of twisted God are you?* Thoughts like these might have shot through my paralyzed mind! Frankly, I can't even comprehend this level of testing—the most precious thing Abraham has is now about to be taken away forever. What will he do?

He tells Isaac they're going on a journey. The past twenty-five years of waiting have established an intimacy between Abraham and God, and he is now convinced that God can only be good to him. He is now certain that it's not in God to be anything other than gracious and generous and trustworthy. So Abraham takes Isaac to a mountain and puts him on the altar and raises the knife to offer him as a sacrifice.

Thousands of years later, the writer of Hebrews opens a window into Abraham's hidden thoughts:

> By faith Abraham, when God tested him, offered Isaac as a sacrifice. He who had received the promises was about to sacrifice his one and only son, even though God had said to him, "It is through Isaac that your offspring will be reckoned." Abraham reasoned that God could raise the dead, and figuratively speaking, he did receive Isaac back from death. (Hebrews 11:17–19)

Strategic Scribblings

Journaling Strategy No. 4:
Let adversity become the means of your success.

What is the chief adversity in your life right now, and how might God redeem that and even use it as a vehicle of destiny in your life? Let your heart risk such a thought, and journal the results of that inner journey on the following lines.

Chapter Five

I Can't Do This!

The Spirituality of Falling

I don't wait well.
The "anxious" hits me, steals up from behind
when nothing important seems to be happening.
The rapid passing of my fixed time grips my soul
and I forget the divine glory
in "small things done with great love."
Wait! What has happened to that bush?
—TUCKER RITNER[1]

I was about twelve years old when I took the terrifying and exhilarating plunge of learning to water ski. My muscular development and coordination were slow in coming, but somehow, in between swallowing my body weight in lake water and torpedoing beneath the surface when I forgot to let go of the towrope, I managed to get vertical on the skis. And what a thrill it was.

Amid the barrage of well-intended advice coming from every side, one admonition from my dad stuck, largely because it was the most ridiculous thing I'd ever heard. *If you start to fall, lean into it, not away from it.*

"I'm sorry… I thought you said, 'Lean *into* the fall'!"

"I did!" he declared. "That's the way to keep from falling—lean toward your fall, and you'll come back upright."

I don't have to tell you how preposterous that sounded, but as I was skittering along the water on wobbly skis, I began to tilt. And somehow, before it was too late, I was able to engage my father's advice and lean toward the fall. It was the hardest, most counterintuitive thing I'd ever done. But darned if it didn't work, and to my surprise…up I popped back on my feet again! Astonishing, isn't it?

That experience was such a vivid aha! moment that it never left me, and years later when I was preparing Sunday sermons on some of Jesus' equally counterintuitive counsel, that day on the lake came rushing back with compelling vibrancy.

When our world vibrates and reels suddenly sideways, when

> **Strategy No. 5:**
>
> *Lean into your fall.*

we careen violently into emotional empty space, instinct reacts faster than thought. We grasp desperately at anything that promises to restore control. And sometimes the first option—which might seem the most natural—is the worst thing you can grab on to. Thus the fifth strategy for growing in divine delays is this: lean into your fall.

When we are falling and the surface is rushing up at dizzying speed to meet us in a hard crash, all the natural options are wrong. Two immediate conclusions rush to our consciousness: either God isn't really all that good after all, or he just plain isn't in control. Either he has stopped loving us, or he's simply not big enough to enforce his good intentions. Sometimes these appear to be the only logically consistent interpretations of our present suffering. Don't grab on to either one.

A Two-Thing Life

What a blessing it was for Kellie and me to move our family into our new house. As boxes were unpacked and we gradually felt the shape of the house imprint our lives with its form and function, we were grateful. Finally a short eternity had ended with our being settled for the first time in years. But as we began organizing rooms for eating and writing and sleeping and homeschooling, an old enemy emerged: <u>financial fear</u>. More like terror, actually.

The giant I hoped was dead had merely been sleeping. And now the answer to our prayers served simply to fatten the foe of fear that threatened our checkbook. *God, how is this supposed to work? Are you really in control here, or is this merely optimistic denial? I'm beginning to hear the sucking sound of a whirling vortex just ahead, ready to siphon us into a financial death spiral. A little help, maybe? Anyone?*

In the early months of 2003 the icy fingers of fear began to squeeze my shoulder as I counted the months our money would

last until we arrived at zero. This is precisely the point where waiting seems a mockery of our faith. *You have to do something, and do
it now!* our minds yell at us. In seasons of waiting we have to resist
the urge to get a death grip on something tangible, like holding on
to a piece of sinking debris after falling overboard into a sea of
intangibles.

The survival instinct in the soul is as strong as it is in the physical body. But often our instincts don't serve us well. Only the truth
of who God is can overcome, correct, and redirect our soul's natural survival instincts in the times when outside forces threaten to
take over.

In *Soul Space* I wrote about living a "one-thing life"—a life
grounded in the centrality of passion for God, refusing to let the
distractions and dissipations of the world distract our focus from
the one thing that matters above all. Now I want to talk about a
two-thing life: the two things that flow out of that one-thing preoccupation with God. In the Scriptures we discover the two facets
of God's Person that are most essential to his nature…and the most
sustaining to ours!

The poet-warrior David probed these matters deeply and
repeatedly in the most emotionally honest and soul-expansive book
in the Bible: Psalms. "One thing God has spoken, two things have
I heard: that you, O God, are strong, and that you, O Lord, are loving" (Psalm 62:11–12).

These words from the pen of a man who endured almost
twenty years of betrayal, persecution, fear, and frustration are David's

testimony to us that while he may not have known everything about God, there are two things he figured out. And he staked his life on these two realities: God is powerful, and God is good. End of story. Well, actually it's the *beginning* of the story. If God can be fully powerful and fully good while we're waiting and hurting, then there has to be more to the story than what we see.

Again our perception largely determines how we'll proceed. Either our experience will interpret our convictions, or our convictions will interpret our experience. Our pain can easily paint a picture of the Father as untrustworthy—the furthest thing from the truth. If, however, we analyze the seeming chaos of our circumstances through the grid of God's power and goodness—as David learned to do—then we anchor our souls and avoid shipwreck.

If our heart-truths are not etched imperviously on the blueprints of our souls, the sheeting torrents of life's storms will cause those lines of understanding to blur and run. After the storms we pick up rebuilding our lives by using the chaotic swirl of lines that remain upon those rain-streaked pages. Certainty retreats into the troubled waters of bitter ambivalence or impulsive relativism.

To be sure, we may not understand what we see. As we gather the fragments left behind by the tumult, we may try to compute sovereignty and suffering, glory revealed and glory denied, and come up with two plus two equals five. But rather than doubt the validity of addition, we realize that we have not yet seen all the factors that belong in this equation. This humbles us (a key component of waiting seasons) rather than destroying our moorings.

God regularly pierces the gossamer veil separating this realm from the next, allowing us to peer through tiny holes into that heavenly space where all is true and nothing illusion. Those who hunger and thirst for Kingdom reality find it in unexpected moments and build their convictions upon it. As they build on spiritual reality, they disregard everything they see on this side of the veil that contradicts that reality. It is my conviction that a life set upon the footings of God's kindness and strength will endure any storm and will enable us to rightly interpret the circumstances of waiting. With a firm grasp on both facets of God's character, we can dare to lean into our fall.

I'm not sure we ever become comfortable with the suspended sensation of falling, but knowing that a safety net does exist... somewhere, just beyond the boundaries of our vision...begins to reduce the terror. So perhaps we can come to the place where we flail just a bit less and we relax just a bit more in a condition that resembles a growing trust—a trust that no matter how disoriented or despairing we feel, we will not be destroyed. There are strong arms to catch us. So we can walk again and fall again and be caught again in a dance that right now feels so dark and dangerous.

It's something like pouncing on my six-year-old son in the neighborhood pool and throwing him into the air. Although our cat-and-mouse game is an established piece of our swimming pool liturgy, it rarely fails to elicit in my son a momentary wide-eyed, breathtaking panic before quickly being replaced by noisy, boyish delight. With God's goodness and power in view, it is my hope that we all can move toward a more rapid transition from panic to delight in our tumultuous times of waiting.

Falling touches a primal fear in most of us, but there are others who actually come to like it. They strap a pack onto their backs and fly thousands of feet into the air only to hurl themselves out of a perfectly good airplane to experience the sensation of free fall. Others choose a slightly tamer version in bungee jumping (bungee falling?) or leaping off a high dive or careening down a zip line. The only difference between terror and thrill, it seems to me, is the presence or absence of the parachute or bungee cord, the hands that catch the jumper, just as my hands catch my son in the swimming pool.

New Tests to Pass

Falling well is a learned skill. The next course at Desert University is Fear and Failure. After Kellie and I moved into our house, the fears of financial ruin were difficult to shake, no matter how much I prayed and searched for God's direction. Just then God's voice was so faint and distant as to be indiscernible.

I have to do something, I told myself. For years we had toyed with the idea of starting a side business, something that could help support oneFlesh Ministries. Before our money was entirely gone, I figured I might be able to secure a bank loan and open a small business.

I had a business degree and a good head for numbers, so I

began to contemplate the possibility of opening a small retail venture, a wine store. I realize this might raise a few eyebrows, but at this point Kellie and I already felt we were swimming against the current of mainstream churchdom. We stood for relationships over programs, intimacy over productivity, and simplicity over activity, even Christian activity. Such values are not always welcome in church circles.

Likewise, when we thought about the possibility of starting a business, we leaned toward combining a hobby with a profit-making venture. In prayer and counsel, I perceived that God was saying, "Go for it." So we did.

During the spring I juggled my writing and occasional speaking opportunities with an intensive market analysis of the region leading to a detailed business plan. Eventually I had a thorough presentation to use in seeking a business loan. The next couple of months were spent talking with bankers, looking at commercial space, and navigating government regulations. But despite the considerable cloud of dust I'd kicked up, I had to face reality later that summer when the funding I wanted didn't appear. In the eyes of the lenders, the economy was too uncertain, and I was untested.

As I weighed the prospect of recalibrating my expectations and repackaging my loan request, I felt as if I heard the still, small Voice: "Let it go!" *What! After all that work? After you said I could pursue this thing, just let it go?*

Enter another paradox of the waiting season: God has the right to say things that, in the short run, make absolutely no sense and may even appear contradictory. *Boy, this is going to be fun explaining to people,* I thought. *Yep, God said to do it (and "waste" five months of my life), and now he's saying "stop it." Hmm...*

Despite the nagging embarrassment, I felt relief more than anything else. Although it felt mildly like a failure, I received two comforting and confirming words from close friends. I had made a brief connection with a minister from England who visited our church some months before, and we had struck up a friendship by e-mail. He said he sensed God was preserving our focus on ministry and guarding us from extraneous distractions. Kellie, it turned out, felt the same thing.

Yes, I suppose it would be too normal for us to actually have a steady income! I pondered ruefully. But a spark of anticipation flickered again about what God might be up to. In all honesty, there's an adventure underlying these times of waiting, but we have to receive that unique grace that cuts through the fear in order to begin to enjoy it as such. Directly proportional to my softly rising hope in God, the taunts of my fears began to subside. I still didn't know where this train was headed, the windows were still fogged, but this particular lurch on the tracks helped assure me that at least we were moving. And that brought hope.

Who God Wants to Be for Us

Just as we were closing shop on the wine store plan, Kellie and I headed to Florence, South Carolina, to conduct a marriage retreat—

our first, actually. Marriage had become a prime focus for us as one of the key realms of intimacy that we felt called to speak to with our lives and ministry...primarily, because our own marriage had experienced such a resurrection during our tenure in Colorado. And Florence was going to be the first place we were to address that vision.

With a mixture of excitement and dread, I began preparing the teaching for the retreat. Fortunately, I began preparing by sitting in God's presence for several days, saying, "Here I am, Lord. What do you want to say through us? What is your heart for these people?" In that place of waiting, I began to receive a remarkably clear picture of what God wanted to do and say. The more revelation that flowed, the more confident and expectant I became, until I couldn't wait to arrive and see God show up.

I'd never experienced confidence like this before. And it confirmed perfectly a word of challenge that God was depositing in my heart through the events of that summer: throw off your fear! I was beginning to see just how greatly my timidity constricted the flow of God's purpose in me. How he wanted to express himself in wonderful, even miraculous ways through my life! But I was often hesitant, not wanting to presume upon God, and this lack of confidence had placed a severe bottleneck upon the grace God wanted to release through Kellie and me. Until now.

Just then, another insight from author Graham Cooke reverberated through my consciousness: "God always wants to be something significant for us. What is it that God wants to be for me now that He couldn't be at any other time, in any other way?"[2] The light bulb flashed on, and I could see it. Taste it. Feel it. The joy of God in expressing his heavenly, redemptive fragrance in the earth through a powerless but trusting soul. Through me. A supernatural courage filled my heart that carried me through the marriage retreat and allowed me to deposit his truth from a place of resolute rest. God was *for* me. He delights to show himself strong on my behalf!

At the retreat, marriages were mended and strengthened. A vision and road map for intimacy was laid out for dozens of couples. But I don't think anyone had a clue about the revolutionary shift taking place inside my soul that weekend—how God anchored my life with a new dimension of trust. It was a defining moment in my season of waiting.

WAITING WELL: MARY TREASURES THE WORD IN HER HEART

Every man and woman in history who loved and served God over the long haul learned a thing or two about trust. Perhaps the one woman who learned the most was Mary, the mother of Jesus. Her tests of waiting were unprecedented, her responses unwavering. But one response was consistent: she displayed an unshakable trust that was demonstrated by treasuring the words of God in her heart!

Upon hearing an unfathomable declaration from an angel

named Gabriel—the promise that Mary would conceive super-naturally and bear the Son of God—she committed herself to this thing that she didn't understand. It made no sense, but in her heart she knew it was true. This is trust. This is waiting well.

And wait she did! Each day prior to missing her first period must have felt like a week. The nine months of waiting during pregnancy must have felt like years. We can only imagine the cost of the shame and accusation she and Joseph bore during that time, but they trusted the word of the Lord delivered by the angel. Mary had so little to go on—just a few words of unimaginable promise.

Mary's life was one of stumbling upon piece after piece of the divine puzzle but not being able to put that puzzle fully together for thirty-three years! Years of waiting…and hoping…and trusting. But at those points of inner crisis that surely rushed upon her many times, Mary *leaned into the fall* by one simple act: she "treasured up all these things and pondered them in her heart" (Luke 2:19).

After the angels appeared to the shepherds, and the shepherds rushed to Bethlehem to bow before Mary's infant Son, she meditated upon the promise. Twelve years later the no-longer-boy-but-not-yet-man Jesus stunned his parents by winding up in an intense debate with Jewish scholars. As Jesus began to awaken to his larger identity and purpose, Mary and Joseph were more perplexed than ever. Mary's response? She meditated upon the gradual unfolding of treasured promises.

This speaks of an enormously anchored and secure reality that Mary had cultivated within herself. Confronted by divine interventions that defied human explanation, she refused the temptations to braid these dangerous loose ends into something manageable, something she could control. Only a prevailing trust allows us to rest within so many uncertainties and to go back—time after time, puzzle piece after puzzle piece—to the foundations of our elusive understanding, the words and promises of our Soul Shepherd.

Mary waited with grace. She waited those first twelve years. She waited the next eighteen until Jesus' destiny began to unfold. In fact, we are left to imagine whether the years of pondering trust didn't equip Mary, alone among humans, to discern and instigate the precise moment of Jesus' inaugural miracle at Cana and the release of ministry that followed.

But her waiting didn't end there. Both the "salvation" and the "piercing" of Mary's soul, prophesied by Simon at Jesus' dedication at the Temple, would not manifest themselves for three more years. Three more years of daily trusting God and resting in the same *two things* that sustained King David in his darkest hours—the power and goodness of an all-knowing, all-wise God. Even when Mary experienced her darkest hours, watching her "promise" die, she treasured and she trusted.

And so must we if we would wait well.

Strategic Scribblings

Journaling Strategy No. 5: Lean into your fall.

Where do you feel the terror of falling, that panic of being out of control? What circumstance, relationship, challenge, or temptation elicits your greatest fear? What tangible step can you take to lean into the arms of Jesus as you're falling so that you can find rest?

_____

_____

_____

_____

_____

_____

_____

_____

_____

_____

_____

Chapter Six

Looking for a Yellow Submarine

The Life-Giving Power of Community

And our friends are all on board...
Everyone of us has all we need...
In our yellow submarine.
—JOHN LENNON and
PAUL MCCARTNEY[1]

In the previous chapter I told the story of the first marriage retreat that Kellie and I led. Along with the gift of confidence and trust that God gave us that weekend, we received another gift—that of friendship and community.

This connection had been growing for months actually. When we moved to Greensboro, we had a chance to renew a friendship with Kellie's college roommate, Paige, and her husband, Paul. And after twelve years of being apart, what a renewal it was! We discovered that we shared a common passion for intimacy with God and common values regarding his purposes in the earth. Paul and Paige were also in the midst of a long waiting season, looking for God's promises of blessing and ministry to finally be released.

We asked them to join us as part of a ministry team at that first marriage retreat, and the fellowship we enjoyed both in travel and in the ministry itself was as significant as anything else that took place that weekend. Our deep hunger to live intimately connected with trusted friends—this yearning God had awakened in us in Colorado—was finally taking form before our eyes.

As the Beatles sang so contagiously in the sixties, we do all yearn for a yellow submarine—a place of true togetherness where the qualities of companionship, mutual trust, and adventure all converge in time and geography. So often we sense vague potential in a relationship here or there or perhaps an opportunity lost as someone moves away, but the vision seems to rarely coalesce into reality. And frankly, we rarely pursue such opportunities with vigor and intentionality. We're too busy with lesser things.

When Kellie and I moved back to the Southeast, we began a prayerful search for the people we knew God would add to our lives. We were confident that he would gather a small group of like-minded men and women to become a community in this new town. This kind of relationship is not crafted quickly, but when the desire for intimacy shapes our fundamental identity and purpose, then we have the means of recognizing the people who are being placed in our lives. God is the One who knits hearts together and draws people into a common passion. He is the Architect of community. He builds the submarines and then recruits the crews to run them.

Relationships are the threads that join us together in the fabric of life. But if there is a time and place where relationships are *most* crucial, it is during the times when God waits. Waiting accentuates our interdependence upon others, a truth hard-wired into every soul. In seasons of waiting, our spiritual health is uniquely dependent upon the wisdom and camaraderie of loyal friends. We need folks who can pray with us, cry with us, and sometimes slap us upside the head.

A New Paradigm for Friendship

But have we rightly understood friendship? Is a friend simply someone who has a common interest—a golfing partner or a Bible study buddy? Someone who is fun to hang out with, someone who is like us or who makes us feel good about ourselves? Those elements may be present, but true friendship goes vastly deeper. A wise king named Solomon said it this way: "A friend loves at all times, and a brother is born for adversity" (Proverbs 17:17). My father used to jokingly quote that verse when my brother Josh and I were being "adverse" with one another. But the truth here is unquestionable: times of adversity highlight the redemptive glory of a spiritual brother or sister, a true friend who will help stabilize our souls in times of great turbulence. Relationships are the currency of God's Kingdom.

Solomon continues: "Perfume and incense bring joy to the heart, and the pleasantness of one's friend springs from his earnest counsel" (Proverbs 27:9). Shallow people are capable of offering only shallow counsel, which is the last thing we need when harsh currents are vibrating our little submarine. In fact, turbulent waters show us, more than anything else, the real quality of the people in our life. So the strategy here is simple: choose your crew well.

Strategy No. 6:
Choose your crew well.

Don't just seek out fun people; find deep people. Of course, a friend can be both fun and deep; it is frequently the thoughtful, spiritual folks who are the most fun to be around. They can see the humor as well as the pathos of life and embrace both. The insight ingrained within deep people is matched and balanced by the humility that characterizes their counsel. They neither dominate you nor waffle on truth; instead, they offer you the treasures drawn from their life without manipulation or expectation. This depth invites and rewards your trust.

As Solomon reflected on the quality of friendship, he noted that "wounds from a friend can be trusted, but an enemy multiplies kisses" (Proverbs 27:6). Wow, that's not what we want to hear! And it's not exactly what we tend to look for in friends. Who wants to spend a lot of time with someone who is likely to confront us and challenge us? However, this is precisely the quality that defines true friendship. Encouragement and comfort only have life-imparting value when we know our friend would just as readily rebuke us when necessary. When we know beyond any doubt that we are loved, then we trust the wound that comes from a loving friend's hand.

It's much easier to write those words than to live them. A rebuke tests both parties: Is my friend secure enough in who he or she is to risk giving me a word of unwelcome correction? Am I humble enough to welcome that word into my situation? Proverbs 17:10 cuts to the heart of the matter: "A rebuke impresses a man of discernment more than a hundred lashes a fool." Sometimes I have been the discerning man. Sometimes I've been the fool.

Kellie and I experienced a life-giving example of this dynamic a few months ago when we spent a weekend with Paul and Paige in the mountains. Among the four of us, one person became vulnerable and invited the input of the others. In response, a gentle word of correction came to the surface, the truth of which was recognized and gladly received. The courage and trust on both sides created a setting for growth and freedom all around. An impartation of life will always be the test and confirmation of loving correction.

Love forms the environment for community, but it's not automatic. The hard fact is that love intimidates us. Love feels so big a topic that we're not sure how to get our hands around it. And as one pastor admitted to me recently, we all know intuitively how far short we fall of really loving each other, so we're reluctant to talk about it overtly. But still we must pursue love to have any chance at cultivating real community in our crew.

As an avid student of the obvious, I recently received fresh insight into the connection between love and community. The passage in my *One Year Bible* (which I am diligently compressing into three years) placed 1 Corinthians 12 and 13 together. Reading them back to back highlighted a beautiful truth that I had missed before: the glorious body life and flow of spiritual gifts described in chapter 12 depend on the practice of love described in chapter 13.

Solomon continues: "Do not forsake your friend and the friend of your father, and do not go to your brother's house when disaster strikes you—better a neighbor nearby than a brother far away" (Proverbs 27:10). We often fail to rightly value friendship until we're in a place of crisis. But then, of course, it's too late. Friendship is not summoned on demand; it is carefully nurtured through the good times and then hammered to a steely strength in hard times so that it is resident in our lives.

If you're caught in turbulent times without a trustworthy friend to turn to, there is still hope. First, "there is a friend who sticks closer than a brother" (Proverbs 18:24), and he will never leave you. Plus, he has wisdom in abundance. While it is much easier to hear his wisdom when it's echoed by a flesh-and-blood friend, God will speak to you directly and rescue you. Second, if you know where to look, there are men and women around with the courage and integrity to speak into your life without the benefit of an established friendship. Though not ideal, this can provide the compass you need in a moment when you're disoriented by chaos.

However, I want to challenge the practice of disposable friendships. We live in a disposable society—we change jobs, change cities, and change relationships with dizzying frequency. But that's our culture, not our spiritual DNA. We are designed for lasting relationships—lifelong marriages and, yes, even lifelong friendships. Even as I write this, I hear the low snort of dismissal from many "realists" who would criticize such Pollyanna notions. But I am convinced that community ripens over time and only grows sweet and nourishing in the context of commitment and longevity. We must not be such willing slaves to the dictates of this world's system!

The practice of replacing our friendships as regularly as we replace our wardrobes or automobiles assures us of an untested crew when the inevitable storms arise. And these are just the personal deficits; what about the larger losses? The world itself is supposed to recognize us as Jesus' disciples because of our committed love for one another; this uncommon selflessness will demonstrate the lordship of Christ in a way no preaching can (see John 13:34–35; 17:20–23). However, if our love doesn't last over the long haul, then it has no meaning. If we bail on one another as soon as we encounter difficulty, then we merely reinforce our superficiality. The Kingdom of God requires more of us. And the currents that buffet our submarines—especially in seasons of waiting—require more of us as well.

Most submarines are not piloted well by a rookie crew but by a battle-tested team that has worked together over time, bringing a broad set of skills into cooperative effort to unleash the destiny of the craft. Using this analogy, I'd like to describe five ways in which community—we'll call them life-friends—can tap the unique spiritual potential of waiting seasons.

Life-Friends Help Stabilize the Craft

Waiting can be uniquely disorienting. It stirs up turbulence that rocks our lives and our expectations. And consider the power of our expectations. When Jacob finally married his bride—the object of seven years' devotion—he expected to wake up beside Rachel. Instead, he'd been duped into marrying her sister, Leah. Talk about a crushed expectation! The result was a combination of rage and despair—feelings we, too, experience when our submarine is buffeted and our navigational systems go awry.

This is precisely where trustworthy friends come alongside us and help us set our rudder in reality while we ride out the turbulence and reset our course. When we lose sight of familiar landmarks and doubt our sense of direction, we're tempted to panic and jettison everything we have believed. In the upheaval of the storm, we can question our moral boundaries, our destiny, even God, and foolishly abandon it all to our ruin.

When you learn to scuba dive, you learn that sensory deprivation can induce a similar disorientation. This is why you always dive with a friend. When you begin to observe erratic behavior in your diving partner, you go to him, gently take hold of his arms, and put your face in his. By getting your buddy to focus on you, you communicate several crucial pieces of information: you are not alone, I am okay, and you are okay too. You help your friend slow his breathing, relax, and not do anything stupid.

This is exactly the reality check we need from one another in our seasons of waiting. Our friends communicate to us that we are not alone, that God is still on his throne, being powerfully good on our behalf...even while our senses are redlining. If you have people in your life who will do this for you, and you for them, then you have found something priceless. Steward that relationship with the greatest of care.

A few weeks ago I was having lunch with Rodger, one of my fellow worship leaders. We were talking easily and enjoying one another's company. After commenting upon a few things taking place in his office currently, Rodger proceeded to describe how God had been faithful to him time after time in his business career. One story after another showcased the divine provision and favor of God that redeemed bad situations and brought honor to God. I just sat and listened.

After half an hour of listening to stories of God's redemptive love and goodness, a lightness began to rest upon my heart. Burdens I didn't even know I was carrying were falling away. Even now, weeks later, I get choked up reflecting on the presence of Jesus that flowed from my friend that day. I don't think Rodger was even aware of it as he washed my soul in the fragrance of heaven. That moment of friendship will last for eternity.

It is worth noting that we cannot expect to *find* good friends without the determination to *be* a good friend. While this should be obvious, we can feel a lack of quality connections but still continue our course of superficial, utilitarian relationships that are intrinsically dissatisfying. If you hunger for more friendship in your life but aren't sure where to begin, this is it: begin by giving yourself to others, by being a stabilizing force in their place of turbulence.

Life-Friends Help Us Read the Currents

While we can often describe the turbulence in our lives with great precision, it's much harder to interpret the *meaning* behind those currents with any degree of accuracy. We frequently don't get a handle on the whys of life until later. But I would dispute those who suggest we shouldn't pursue the why question.

Circumstances that have no meaning attached are inherently meaningless. Life is a mystery, to be sure, but it's a mystery to be pursued, not abandoned in passivity. Not relegated to the hereafter. Not chalked up to the theological cop-out of God's sovereignty. The very real sovereignty and transcendence of God that awe us also invite us to peer behind the veil, from "glory to glory," toward ever-increasing revelation of meaning until we stand face to Face.

A passage from 1 Corinthians explores this mysterious interplay between what is hidden and what is revealed: "As it is written: 'No eye has seen, no ear has heard, no mind has conceived what God has prepared for those who love him'—but God has revealed it to us by his Spirit. The Spirit searches all things, even the deep things of God.... We have not received the spirit of the world but the Spirit who is from God, that we may understand what God has freely given us" (1 Corinthians 2:9–10, 12).

We would have no clue on how to interpret the intentions of God except that God planted his Holy Spirit within us to reveal his heart so we would understand! Yet the Spirit does not reside only in individuals; he also resides within the community. As we engage life with friends, we often hear from God in ways we never could when we're alone. Friends can perceive more clearly where we are and why, because they aren't enmeshed in our questions and struggles. This is God's cunning way of drawing us into the beauty of community.

A proverb lays open the crucial issue: "A man's steps are directed by the LORD. How then can anyone understand his own way?" (20:24). How indeed? God is directing a much larger drama than we can see from here, so how can we make sense of our part in it? The answer lies in community. No, our friends won't always have the complete answer. But they will frequently be God's mouthpiece to provide crucial perspectives, fellowship, understanding, and intercession during turbulent times. And that is a precious gift, one only available to those who have cultivated life-friends.

LIFE-FRIENDS HELP US UPGRADE OUR EQUIPMENT

One benefit of facing turbulence is that it shows where our equipment is insufficient. Maybe we're relying upon obsolete technology. In other words, the methods we used in past seasons to navigate life and understand God are no longer adequate. The current waiting season is a time for refurbishing or replacing outmoded navigational techniques. New faith is needed perhaps, or a new level of discernment. Spiritual gifts are being activated that have lain dormant within us, untested and unused.

In times like these, God raises up a friend or some other resource to provide the equipping that we can't provide for ourselves. Since God has determined that we will never be self-sufficient (cowboy mentalities notwithstanding), we should look to the trusted ones in our lives to help us identify and upgrade our deficiencies.

Kellie helped upgrade my equipment recently. We were discussing Henri Nouwen's *Can You Drink the Cup?* in which he described the communal potency of lifting the cup around the table, of offering a toast, of savoring the sacred gift of life and family and purpose. Tears gathered in Kellie's eyes as we realized we had botched a unique opportunity the evening before. We had entertained family members at our table, including Kellie's brother and his wife from France…all without honoring the handiwork of God in our lives.

The revelation penetrated my heart that, in general, I have squandered countless family times around the table. I tend to quietly enjoy my food while listening to others talk. But my calling from God as head of my precious family is to recognize and seize opportunities for blessing, for instruction, for love. I grieved and repented my lack of leadership and reached out for fresh equipping from the Father to become this kind of man. Without Kellie's assistance, this equipping would not have occurred.

Times of waiting prior to being released in our destiny form opportune moments to study Scripture, read books on strategic topics, or receive counseling so that we can dispatch baggage from our past. Sharpen your spiritual gifts through use and critique; seek mentoring in the field of your calling. Friends can help you grow and develop in areas related to your ultimate purpose. Identify your faulty equipment, and ask friends for perspective, advice, and resources to make this season count.

LIFE-FRIENDS HELP MAN THE TORPEDOES

We don't just coast through the waters of life unchallenged. The enemies of our soul are real and dangerous, which is a big reason we need one another so desperately. It's hard to pilot the craft and load the torpedoes at the same time. Life-friends frequently can identify the enemy more accurately than we can. That's not to say that we can shirk responsibility for our own issues, but it often takes a shared defense to repel the enemy.

As I was writing those words, I noticed a chipmunk and a small bird squabbling about ten feet outside my window. The bird was trying to drive the chipmunk away, but the chipmunk was simply ignoring the bird. It was most amazing. The bird would stand about a foot away and then dart over to whack the striped rodent with its tiny feet, while the furry intruder just nosed around in the grass looking for a snack. I don't know what the bird was trying to protect, perhaps its nest. But the chipmunk, who was about the size of the bird, was impervious to the winged attacks.

Then suddenly the persevering bird was joined by its mate, who swooped from the sky and made a run at the critter. This time, in a stunning about-face, the chipmunk streaked away for the protection of the nearest rhododendron bush with the two birds on its tail. One bird didn't even faze its enemy, but the instant it was joined by its companion the tables were turned. Astonishing.

In the movie *Gladiator,* Maximus manages to outlive the other gladiators due to his ability to harness his companions into a unified team against their opponents. Those who engaged their foes one-on-one were quickly dispatched. In contrast, Maximus taught his friends how to bring their shields together in a wall of defense and then attack the enemy in concert. Every villain was defeated because of the quality of community he developed.

Through our commitment to one another, we can spot the strategies of the Evil One—discouragement, self-pity, isolation, addiction—and go to war on behalf of our friends. We can sound the alarm; we can counsel; we can pray; we can simply be present. Paul instructed the Thessalonians how to function in this way: encourage one another, respect them, warn them, help the weak, be patient, be kind, be joyful, pray continually, give thanks, test everything, avoid evil (see 1 Thessalonians 5:11–22). Being a true friend is demanding—it requires much of the one giving and the one receiving. But it is life!

Life-Friends Help Move Us Toward Our Destiny

Finally, the core relationships of our community function as a rudder, helping us identify distractions and keeping us oriented in the direction of our destiny. The compulsion to constantly pick up new tasks can easily deceive us, luring us toward goals that force us off course. False goals may not be evil, per se, but they can readily divert us from our true direction. Friends help us stay focused and committed to the larger will of God.

I have known for some years that I am fashioned for intimacy, that this is the overarching purpose of my life. But over the past few months I've had the defining realization that intimacy is *time-*

consuming. It doesn't fit easily around larger jobs and occupations. It is, in fact, an occupation in its own right.

This accounts for my ongoing sense of frustration over the lack of visible "productivity" in my life. Now I'm reframing my understanding of my life, realizing that I have two part-time "jobs." I'm called to spend roughly half my time cultivating spiritual intimacy with God and with my core community. That's my first job. And it qualifies me to undertake the second, which is ministry to others. My writing, speaking, and worship leading are meaningless without the validating foundation of intimacy. This is essential to who Jerome Daley is and is becoming.

This growing conviction in my soul is flourishing because so many others are speaking into it. My wife, my pastor, and at least three close friends have this year confirmed this reality for my destiny. This is a keeping power I never could have obtained on my own. It causes me to stay the course when the terrors of turbulence strike. And strike they will.

Waiting Well: David Draws Deeply upon His Community

David, the ancient poet-warrior of Israel, experienced the terrors of turbulence. In one form or another, he lived through the turbulence of waiting for more than twenty-four years.

He was perhaps thirteen years old when the rivulets of Samuel's anointing oil ran down his beardless face and proclaimed a destiny beyond belief. Kingship. Glory. Wealth and honor. But the road from baptism to breakthrough led, once again, through the desert —the searing, mocking antithesis of his ultimate destiny.

In year five, Saul, the king David would replace, sent his army once again to hunt David down and kill him. This deadly pursuit dragged on year after year. One scheme after another. Ten years in the desert, and David was still playing a dangerous game of cat and mouse, this time with the Philistine king—feigning loyalty to him in order to survive the murderous plotting of Saul. Fifteen years... more of the same. How does destiny survive such time and trouble and turbulence as this?

David was able to stabilize his soul, interpret his circumstances, and keep moving toward his destiny partly because he harnessed the power of community. If he had been alone, I think his chances for obtaining the promised kingship would have been razor thin. But beginning with his extended family, David gathered others around him who shared his plight—a dozen here, a dozen there, until four hundred men banded together in this rough desert fellowship.

Of course, David could not have a close friendship with four hundred people. Besides his two wives, he had a group of thirty "mighty men"—valiant warriors who probably knew David the best. Of these thirty, there were three who enjoyed a uniquely intimate relationship with him (see 2 Samuel 23:8–11). But there was clearly no individual who shared David's life as did his unlikely friend Jonathan, the son of Saul, David's archenemy. This legendary relationship formed the backbone of David's resolve and endurance throughout so lengthy a waiting time.

Jonathan performed all the vital functions of friendship for David in times of crisis. He equipped him (see 1 Samuel 18:4), defended him (19:4–6), stabilized him (20:1–4), moved him toward his destiny (20:12–17), and interpreted events around him (20:24–42). Perhaps more than any other biblical relationship, we see the empowering potential of friendship realized between these two men. As a result, David harnessed his waiting season and made it the servant of his destiny.

At the age of thirty, David finally became king.

Strategic Scribblings

Journaling Strategy No. 6: Choose your crew well.

How deep and wide have you cultivated intimacy with your "crew"? Are you allowing them to serve you in your season of waiting? Are your close friends stabilizing, interpreting, equipping, defending, and holding you on course? Are you doing the same for them?

Chapter Seven

The Night Must End

Avoiding Heartsickness While Waiting

Since ancient times no one has heard,
no ear has perceived, no eye has seen
any God besides you, who acts on behalf
of those who wait for him.

—ISAIAH 64:4

I t was November 2003, a year and a half since we had returned to North Carolina, and I was invited to lead worship at the church where I had spent ten years as worship pastor. A complex blend of emotions churned inside me as I prepared to take the stage, more than three years since I had last been there. The warmth of familiarity. A bit of nervousness. The recognition that, as Jesus observed, prophets are not usually welcome in their hometowns.

Not that I was a prophet exactly, and not that I wasn't welcomed. It's just that people who have known you for a long time…well, they think they know you. But when you tap into your destiny, you become a new person in a very real sense, and old friends or family members sometimes resist that newness on a subconscious level. They want you to be the person you *used* to be because it feels more safe or familiar.

Still, everyone was wonderfully warm and entered into worship enthusiastically. Afterward, as I was shaking hands and trading hugs, one close friend hung back to let the crowd thin. Then he approached me with both a smile and a penetrating gaze. "How are you? Really?" he asked, knowing we only had a few minutes to get real. "How's the writing? How's ministry?"

I responded with vague generalities, not because I wanted to hide anything, but because there wasn't much to tell. "Yep, doin' some writing. Doin' a little speaking here and there."

"Ah, still waiting, eh?" he nodded knowingly.

I started to agree but paused. A ray of revelation warmed me suddenly, and I saw in an instant that it didn't feel like waiting any longer. Not that anything external had changed in the last months, but I realized that something inside me had altered. I groped to understand the new feeling. There was still waiting ahead—I knew that much—but the sensation of waiting had shifted from center stage to backstage. In its place was a new sense of movement and purpose.

It was a subtle change, but real. The circumstances in my life—both what was present and what was lacking—were beginning to reflect meaning. The inner revolution of confidence at the retreat, the store option failing, my increasing role in our new church's worship—all these pieces seemed to be saying something. Something like, *Your life is not as chaotic and aimless as you sometimes feel. I am up to something. Things are working together for a good purpose. Just keep on keeping on, and watch it unfold.* It was as intangible as a breath of air, but that breath warmed my soul and began to change my perspective.

When we focus on waiting, it's like watching a pot of water before it boils. We try to tear our eyes away, but our anxious hearts return again and again, trying to anticipate the exact moment at which our lives will boil over into destiny. We can be as squirmy and restless as a seven-year-old boy trying to survive a long-winded preacher. (I know this from both ends!) But when waiting ceases to be the object of our attention, we experience a powerful liberation. It's a vital moment of transition, and in that instant of conversation with my friend, I saw it and realized I had crossed over. A mild victory perhaps, but a victory nonetheless.

"No, I'm not waiting, exactly," I told him. "I'm moving. And it feels good!"

JOSHUA'S SPIRITUAL WARFARE

Joshua was familiar both with waiting and with movement. No, not that Joshua. Not the guy who brought down Jericho, but a guy who lived about seven hundred years later. This Joshua was the high priest during the rebuilding of Zerubbabel's Temple, described in the books of Ezra and Nehemiah. It's a phenomenal story, a story of successful waiting! But you can decide for yourself.

The year is 536 BC. Ezra has just orchestrated, under the blessing of the Persian king Cyrus, the return of fifty thousand excited Israelites to rebuild Jerusalem and the Temple of God. Zerubbabel is the new governor. Zechariah and Haggai are the resident prophets.

The people dive into their work with vigor, sorting through the burned rubble and weathered stones of their past glory, preparing the site for the new Temple, and laying the foundation with precision. The promises of God fill their hearts as they labor and sweat. They are living out the destiny spoken so long before by the prophet Jeremiah:

> This is what the LORD says: "When seventy years are completed for Babylon, I will come to you and fulfill my gracious promise to bring you back to this place. For I know the plans I have for you," declares the LORD, "plans to prosper you and not to harm you, plans to give you hope and a future. Then you will call upon me and come and pray to me, and I will listen to you. You will seek me and find me when you seek me with all your heart. I will be found by you," declares the LORD, "and will bring you back from captivity. I will gather you from all the nations and places where I have banished you," declares the LORD, "and will bring you back to the place from which I carried you into exile." (Jeremiah 29:10–14)

For seventy years that promise of God hung in the air, bringing hope to some and despair to others. But now, finally, the word was coming to pass! Their confidence in God rocketed as they watched the promise take shape slowly before their very eyes. But it's interesting that the generation enjoying the fulfillment of God's promise was not the generation that had endured seventy years of waiting. The new generation had not yet had the chance to experience the transforming, qualifying power of promises that are tested by time.

But that was soon to change. The people who had occupied the land during Israel's exile were less than thrilled to see this shift in "their" territory. Scrambling to retain their power base, they curried favor with the new Persian king, Artaxerxes, and poisoned his mind regarding the Temple project. Work was forcibly halted. The Israelites reluctantly went back to the mundane business of living ...and waiting.

Months passed with no movement. A year, and no change in the royal decree. The passion that had burned so brightly and seemed so imminent was now callously torn from their grasp. What could God be thinking? Didn't he care? Was he not vested in performing his own promises?

Deferred Hope

There is a proverb that describes this dilemma with great accuracy: "Hope deferred makes the heart sick" (Proverbs 13:12). We're familiar with things that are deferred. Just about every day I receive offers of new credit accounts, sometimes with deferred payments! Tempting my baser appetite for instant gratification, the offer occasionally moves me to indulge in a moment of what-if, envisioning the rush of quick pleasure I could have in an instant...and defer the pain of paying the price until later. Hmm...

But hope deferred is just the opposite. In a sinister twist, the pain comes now while I wait for a pleasure that seems to have no date of arrival. And heartsickness is the frequent result. Has your heart gone there? Have you struggled with a creeping cynicism, a bitterness of mind, trying perhaps to dull the pain with credit-induced pleasures and deferred payments?

My own heart was feeling the effects of this sickness when Kellie and I decided to take our kids to Chicago for our oldest daughter's birthday. Both our girls had become enamored with American Girl dolls and all the doll-related paraphernalia that the company plied with zealous efficiency through the mail. You can get clothes and accessories and furniture and even tiny dolls for the dolls. Yes, your doll can have a doll of its own. Since one of the American Girl retail stores was in Chicago, we decided to make the pilgrimage. Once we got there, we noticed signs for the Chicago engagement of the Broadway hit *The Lion King*. What a neat experience *that* would be for the kids!

Although our discounted tickets placed us partially behind some pillars, we settled down in the gorgeous old theater to enjoy the show. From the first note, we were whisked away into an exotic, magical story. But entranced as I was by the stunning costumes and primal music, I wasn't prepared for the impact of the story itself. The searing guilt and alienation of the young Simba, driven from his home by forces beyond his control, became my own. The confused panic and then the dull emptiness of a lost destiny loomed over him—and me—with suffocating desolation.

I was gripped by Simba's heartsickness as he agonized over the abandonment he felt as a result of his father's death. We know this feeling, because at times our Father can seem so very far away. During the play, in the midst of that blackness, a throb of percussion sounded as a choir began to sing—faintly but with feeling—and gradually swelled until it filled the room.

> I know that the night must end…
> I know that the clouds must clear…
> I know, yes, I know, the sun will rise![1]

Hot tears splashed down my face as my throat tightened in a muffled sob. Yes, the night must end; it won't last forever. Daybreak will come for me. Kellie and I won't be lost forever in this foggy shroud. The Son will break through, and the sweetness of our purpose will erase the memory of all our heartsickness.

Joshua the Homeless

Back in the ruins of Jerusalem, the heartsickness had not yet broken for Joshua, the high priest. Joshua the Homeless would have been a more appropriate title for him at that moment. *A priest with no temple is a bit of a sham, isn't it?* he probably mused. *Like a snail without a shell! All I am is a slug.* And into his deep, blue funk the Lord broke through with the voice of the prophet Zechariah. And the light of God's revelation brought meaning out of his darkness.

> Then he showed me Joshua the high priest standing before the angel of the LORD, and Satan standing at his right side to accuse him. [*Whoa! What's he doing here? Oh yeah…he's the Accuser.*] The LORD said to Satan, "The LORD rebuke you, Satan! The LORD, who has chosen Jerusalem, rebuke you! Is not this man a burning stick snatched from the fire?" (Zechariah 3:1–2)

Can you imagine a prophet of God walking up and painting this picture for you? This is heavy stuff. But the prophet encouraged Joshua with three moments of illumination that shed light on our own heartsickness during this season of waiting.

Illumination No. 1: You Are Being Accused!

The Enemy takes advantage of our waiting seasons. In the midst of our vulnerability, he plants lie after lie. We shrug off the first one and maybe the second one. But eventually we get worn down and begin to agree with his accusations. Don't accept that garbage!

It starts like this: *You are in pain, and pain is bad. Something must be wrong! God's promises work for other people but not for you. You don't have enough faith. Plus you don't always have a quiet time, so how can God ever use you?*

And if the accusations don't focus on you, they turn to somebody else. *Your pastor is holding you back. He doesn't trust you. You would be moving in power and anointing if he would just give you a chance!*

Or the Accuser points the finger at God. *God must not care about all your suffering, or he would do something about it. He is all-powerful, right? So why is he just standing idly by while your life is going down the drain?*

Into Joshua's condition—and ours—the Lord moves swiftly and decisively to uproot the Enemy's lie. We bear his name, his power, and his authority in prayer as we reject the Accuser: "The Lord rebuke you, Satan! The Lord has chosen *(insert your name)* and has carved out a redemptive destiny for me! God has already begun a good work in me, and he will complete it." The Enemy has no recourse when we position ourselves inside the divine purpose; his lies break apart and dissolve.

Illumination No. 2: Look at What You're Wearing!

Once the lie's grip on our mind is exposed and dealt with, the Lord moves on to address our identity. Just as he did with Joshua, who was dressed in filthy clothes as he stood before the angel of the Lord.

> The angel said to those who were standing before him, "Take off his filthy clothes." [*His old identity!*]
>
> Then he said to Joshua, "See, I have taken away your sin, and I will put rich garments on you."

Then I said, "Put a clean turban on his head." So they
put a clean turban on his head and clothed him [*his new
identity!*], while the angel of the LORD stood by. (Zechariah
3:4–5)

Go ahead. Get rid of that old identity! The person who knows
and owns what God has done for him and has assumed the new
identity—that of a chosen son or daughter rather than a Kingdom
stowaway—is prepared to join the Father in seasons of waiting
with anticipation and partnership.

This is another gift of the waiting season: it tends to expose
what we really believe about God and ourselves. And this is pivotal
to our quest. Instead of living under the shame of failed performance, we embrace the liberating reality of passionate ownership.
We no longer have to prove ourselves. We're now free to accept the
mind-bending, heart-healing love of the Father and the destiny he
has chosen for us.

Illumination No. 3: Embrace the Purpose of God over Your Life!

God's intention for you is even bigger and more wonderful than
you know! Have the courage to embrace your destiny! Zechariah's
vision continues:

The angel of the LORD gave this charge to Joshua: "This is
what the LORD Almighty says: 'If you will walk in my ways

and keep my requirements, then you will govern my house and have charge of my courts, and I will give you a place among these standing here.

"'Listen, O high priest Joshua and your associates seated before you, who are men symbolic of things to come: I am going to bring my servant, the Branch. See, the stone I have set in front of Joshua! There are seven eyes on that one stone, and I will engrave an inscription on it,' says the LORD Almighty, 'and I will remove the sin of this land in a single day.

"'In that day each of you will invite his neighbor to sit under his vine and fig tree,' declares the LORD Almighty." (Zechariah 3:6–10)

The first thing we notice here is that God's promises to us are conditional: we have to hold our bearing and not give up the quest. Perseverance allows us to partner with God in seeing his purposes accomplished in and through us. We can't give up!

Second, our lives are symbolic of the Kingdom that God is bringing to earth. (In the angel's words to Joshua, the Branch, the stone, and the seven eyes are biblical allusions to God's Kingdom.) Both our response to waiting and our participation in destiny are to shine with the glory of that Kingdom rule, and in that way we can demonstrate the heart of God now in our waiting, long before the promise is completed.

Third, God intends to restore what is broken, not only in us individually but also corporately, resulting in a heavenly community. This is the larger Story we are living in!

Strategy No. 7:
Adopt the Joshua paradigm: cut off, change, and confirm.

Let's synthesize this prophetic word and apply it to our situation. What are God's instructions for us in the midst of our waiting? In short, we are to cut off, change, and confirm. Cut off the Enemy's accusations over our lives. Change the clothes of our identity. And confirm the purposes of God that are far beyond anything we can imagine.

Waiting Well: Zerubbabel Learns Not to Despise Small Beginnings

The high priest Joshua wasn't the only person struggling with discouragement while the Temple foundation lay desolate. Thousands who had invested their sweat and time and hope in this vision had to wrestle with God for the meaning of this divine delay, including a man named Zerubbabel, the governor of the new Israelite colony.

Every year the fledgling nation celebrated the special feasts—Passover, the Day of Atonement, the Feast of Booths. Each was a declaration of God's faithful provision in the past. Meanwhile the bare foundation of the Temple mocked these celebrations and the faith of the Jews who honored God's faithfulness. One year passed. Five years. Ten years went by without even a glimmer of the fulfillment of God's promise.

In mercy, the Lord again sent a word of hope through Zechariah, but this time to Zerubbabel.

> So he said to me, "This is the word of the LORD to Zerubbabel: 'Not by might nor by power, but by my Spirit,' says the LORD Almighty.
>
> "What are you, O mighty mountain? Before Zerubbabel you will become level ground. Then he will bring out the capstone to shouts of 'God bless it! God bless it!'"
>
> Then the word of the LORD came to me: "The hands of Zerubbabel have laid the foundation of this temple; his hands will also complete it. Then you will know that the LORD Almighty has sent me to you.
>
> "Who despises the day of small things? Men will rejoice when they see the plumb line in the hand of Zerubbabel."
> (Zechariah 4:6–10)

Zerubbabel received this encouragement deep into his soul and used its truth to wait well. First, he welcomed the comforting reminder that God is unequivocally in charge! God will accomplish his purposes in his time and in his way. There is no obstacle that can deter him. This conviction has to be constantly reinforced on the heart level. So, although it appeared that God's plan had been stymied by Israel's enemies, they were simply pawns in a game whose outcome was already determined. This is the weight of sovereignty in the lives of God's children!

Second, Zerubbabel embraced his own personal role in the

fulfillment of God's plan. The Temple wouldn't just be built some-day by someone. Oh no! No one but Zerubbabel would lay the fin-ishing stone in place and preside over the completion of the promise.

Finally, the governor allowed his perspective to change so that he could begin to see things in the same way God sees. *Don't despise the day of small things!* Appearances can be deceiving. Nineteen years of waiting appeared to be a major failure, but they were not! In God's all-encompassing wisdom, these years became part of the shaping influence that qualified these men and women to take their place in the divine purpose.

And it happened. A new Persian king came to power. New favor and new provision followed. And the Temple was completed. Twenty years of waiting paid off, and destiny became reality.

Strategic Scribblings

Journaling Strategy No. 7:
Adopt the Joshua paradigm: cut off, change, and confirm.

Think about the things that are making you heartsick right now. Then list the Enemy's accusations that have crept into your mind. Now *cut them off* in prayer. Ask God to show you what clothes you are wearing. Then ask him to *change* you into your true identity. Finally, let God *confirm* his good intentions over your life, and write them down on the lines that follow.

_____

_____

_____

_____

_____

_____

_____

_____

_____

_____

_____

_____

Chapter Eight

Staying Power

Guarding Your Integrity

> Yes, there is a "secret to happiness"—
> and it is gratitude.
> All happy people are grateful,
> and ungrateful people cannot be happy.
> —DENNIS PRAGER[1]

The jangle of the phone startled me out of my reverie. I leaned across my desk and checked the caller ID. It was Chris, my new worship collaborator.

I reached eagerly for the phone, anticipating the first real practice for our new band and the excitement that lay ahead. No telling where God might take this team of quality guys. For no less than eight years, God had been speaking to me about his desire to use my musical calling in ways that far exceeded anything I'd been able to do as a worship pastor. I knew he wanted me to write songs and lead young people into the manifest presence of God.

But I hadn't seen it yet.

The promise was so big that it intimidated me greatly. It hadn't been until about three years earlier that I had begun to see God (and myself) with enough clarity to trust that he could accomplish this thing. Even then, as I would try to write a song, the Accuser would laugh at me. *This is pathetic. Your lyrics are tired and trite; your music is flat.*

Kellie remained faithful to the vision and regularly encouraged me. But for a time I'd just snap back at her. "Don't talk to me about the *new sound*. I'm sick of thinking about it. Sick of trying to make it happen."

Jaded. Disappointed. Even a bit angry and cynical. These emotions were gnawing on me. And these are the pitfalls of waiting. In these times the promises of God rose up to almost torment me with their intrusive absence. The Old Testament character Joseph faced this same torment while waiting for his own promise to materialize. In fact, Joseph experienced it so keenly that hundreds of years later King David wrote about it: "Until the time that his word came to pass, the word of the LORD tested him [Joseph]" (Psalm 105:19, NASB). It's like that word is a fire beneath us, provoking us, building the heat on us, threatening to burn us…or perhaps purify us. It's like a pebble in our shoe that irritates and chafes and raises a blister.

But the phone call from Chris reminded me that the chafing was giving way to fulfillment. Or at least the *hope* of fulfillment.

For a couple of months my expectation for musical movement had grown without any clear reason. Then, as Chris and I and our wives talked, we sensed this was a unique convergence of calling and opportunity. We started making plans for a band. It was only a start, but it was movement in the right direction.

As Chris's voice broke across the line, we chatted for a few minutes. Then, during a pause in the conversation, he bravely plunged in. "You know, Jerome, I've had a growing uneasiness about this."

Thinking he was talking about a potential band member, I inquired casually, "Oh? What are you thinking?"

"It's the band thing. Somehow it's just not feeling quite right. (Pause) I think we need to back up a little and wait on this."

As his words began to settle, the sudden loss swept over me. I tried to recover and sound calm. "Oh." I paused, trying to find my wits in the riptide. "Okay… Wow…that's a bit, um, disappointing. Still, I'm glad you spoke up. We'll just, uh, see where God takes us from here."

My hand limply hung up the receiver, and I leaned back in stunned silence. *O God…I thought you were finally breaking in, finally starting to move me toward one piece of my destiny. What are you doing to me?*

OUT OF THE FRYING PAN

The temperature control on the oven of testing moved suddenly from a simmering 250 to a roasting 400. The heat rocked me with baffling, disconnected emotions. It's here that we find what integrity means and just how far ours extends. Cars are tested for structural integrity by subjecting them to the harshest conditions possible—extremes of hot and cold, rugged washboard roads, wind tunnels, and G-force turns. If our souls can sustain the same battery without cracking or quitting, then the integrity is there.

Integrity is staying power. Integrity is consistency. Integrity is character empowered for good things after passing the test of bad things.

Psychologist and author Gerald May offers a refreshingly candid perspective:

> I must confess that I am no longer very good at telling the
> difference between good things and bad things.... From the
> standpoint of inner individual experience the distinction
> has become blurred for me. Some things start out looking
> great but wind up terribly, while other things seem bad in
> the beginning but turn out to be blessings in disguise....
> At some point, I gave up trying to decide what's ultimately
> good or bad. I truly do not know.[2]

Integrity, it seems to me, is one of the good things that comes out of the bad things that test us. Things, be they good or bad or any shade in between, happen to us every day, but every one of them can have redemptive value, tempering the metal of our integrity.

I didn't hold Chris responsible for breaking up my vision for the band. I knew he was doing his best to listen to God. And I suppose that was a first test of my integrity, not to take offense at the people involved in my testing. By the grace of God, Chris and I continued to share fellowship and occasional music making.

The second test was to refuse to throw in the towel on the whole promise of being in a band. I could easily have said, "Okay, God, you fooled me once, but I'm not going to let you do it again. I'm outta here!" But a promise is a promise, and I'm too stubborn to let go. Somehow, sometime, God will use my musical calling in a new way, in some form that is bigger than anything I can cook up. Ironically, it was in the aftermath of that shock wave that I began to see the seeds of musical promise for the future. But I'm still waiting on it.

In times of testing, when we are tempted to think God has stopped moving in our life, God uses three tools to enhance our integrity. We are empowered by remembrance, gratitude, and vigilance.

The Power of Remembrance

Often, when the fires of testing are kindled around us, Satan uses an odd weapon against us—our propensity to forget. Our memory dims, and we lose the force of all that God has done for us in the past. There is no more securing anchor in the storm than our personal experiences of God's actual redemption in our lives, yet we tend to steward these priceless possessions poorly.

Nevertheless, God continues to break into our world in ways large and small, never taking a break and never leaving us to our own devices. When we stop and think about it, we can point back to pivotal times in our lives, places where heaven intersected earth with defining power for our identity and calling. But in the thick of the pain of refining, these heavenly benchmarks appear far removed from our present dilemma. Still, if we can press through the struggle and recapture those deposits of grace from our history, we will be richly rewarded. Reviewing God's past goodness and involvement in our hearts brings the stability and refreshment we need day after day.

The Power of Gratitude

Remembrance leads us directly into thanksgiving, and thanksgiving has power like little else to cut through confusion and intimidation. Psalm 50:23 unwraps a potent truth: "He who sacrifices thank offerings honors me, and he prepares the way so that I may show him the salvation of God." In other words, as gratitude flows from our lips, the glory of God is magnified. And as God's beauty and wonder are elevated, his redemptive power is released to deliver us from difficulty. Not that the waiting automatically ceases, but grace is imparted so we can move purposefully forward through the desert and toward our destiny.

In the heat of testing, these tools are the difference between life and death. God has equipped us with all we need, more than enough to hold the course. Many of God's people fall and die in the desert while forgotten, life-saving provisions are tied to their camels just a step away. We can't afford to join them; we can't afford to ignore the provision of God.

The Power of Vigilance

The noble centaur in C. S. Lewis's beloved Narnia books remarked to the sturdy old badger, "It is mine to watch as it is yours to remember,"[3] offering us another insight into the characteristics of integrity. Integrity remembers. And integrity watches.

Watches for what? Watches for movement. Watches for meaning. Gerald May reflects, "All too often…our preoccupation with finding relief [leaves] little opportunity to look for meaning."[4] Integrity moves us beyond the search for soul relief and toward the search for meaning. No event or feeling, no circumstance or matter of waiting is without meaning, and yet the meaning of these things is frequently hidden. A vigilant heart, however, will keep us attuned to God and to the Kingdom dynamics surrounding us so we can patiently take hold of meaning as it emerges.

> **Strategy No. 8:**
> *Leverage your integrity through remembrance, gratitude, and vigilance.*

Integrity watches the natural realm and the spiritual realm for telltale signs of Kingdom clash, allowing us to take our position strategically and redemptively.

SOFTENING THE HEART

Waiting seasons tend to push us one way or the other. Either they harden our hearts or soften them. Of course, softer is better.

In the past few months I've been surprised by the grace God has brought—unbidden, I might add—for repentance. *Repentance,* what a foreboding word! Distasteful at best. Something to be avoided unless entirely necessary. But I had forgotten just how sweet that fruit is…until recently.

In the course of a recent Sabbatical, God elicited in me a surprise discovery. Kellie and I were talking, and I admitted something I had just then realized. God was displeased with a certain attitude I harbored.

I'd been observing the growing phenomenon of Christian fads, books particularly, that sweep across the church landscape with unstoppable buzz. Every cutting-edge church jumps on the bandwagon, rushing to offer the new pulpit series or small-group method. Every believer in the know has read the book and is talking the new lingo. This obsession to be in sync with the marketing forces seems to drown out the unique things God is saying or doing in the life of each church. And while the books that occasion these fads generally have good content, the trend itself disturbs me.

But when God put his finger on this attitude in me, he was getting at something deeper. My attitude toward church fads had led me to view celebrity authors negatively, and I realized God was not happy about it. Kellie probed deeper. "Are you sure this isn't simple jealousy?" she asked. I'm not sure how much I hemmed and hawed before admitting, first to myself and then to her, that this was precisely my condition.

So far so good. Between the Holy Spirit and Kellie, my sin had been flushed from its hiding place. But *it* hadn't happened yet— the actual transformation of my heart that I desired. I began to pray—that's what you do with sin. You confess it, ask for forgiveness, and receive grace to change. And suddenly, in the midst of my earnest but somewhat mechanical processing, the Holy Spirit did *it*. A deep grief welled up inside me, and I saw—really saw and felt—how far I had fallen. I had fallen from the grace of thinking well of people, wishing people well, and had instead secretly envied their success. How I had robbed the glory of God by my own self-interest and self-promotion! It cut me to the heart, and I wept.

Strangely, this experience of grief and remorse was the most tender and intimate of moments with the Lover of my soul. Interwoven with my brokenness was a deep joy and sense of being tended by God—that I was so precious to him as to warrant his personal cultivation in my heart, weeding out the thorns that were choking my life and setting me free to love again.

As I reflected on the experience later, I tried to remember the last time I had cried over my own sin. I'm ashamed to say I couldn't find it in my memory. But my waiting season had offered me this rich fruit to nourish my soul and establish my character more wholly. Over the next weeks God brought me back again to different situations he wanted to address, and again I knew that glorious rending of heart and deep cleansing of soul. This is the shaping and molding of integrity that can take place during our times of waiting unlike any other time.

AFTERSHOCKS

In the weeks after God rudely interrupted my musical hopes, I gradually found rest and trust again, vaguely sensing the wisdom of God in plotting my course through these strange twists and turns. Now a third test was appearing. The first test was my relationship with Chris, the second was my relationship with God, but the third test was more difficult to define. I just felt it.

It was probably a month later, and I began to notice a lot of "soul junk" bubbling up and floating around inside. Unsettledness. Discontentment. Tides of depression. Stabs of anger. *What's going on?* I wondered. *Where is this stuff coming from?* As I got quiet and listened to my heart and the Holy Spirit, I realized these were aftershocks from the soulquake of that phone call. I had tidied up all the issues on the surface, but the subterranean repercussions were just now being felt.

If you have weathered a soulquake in your season of waiting, you also may need to examine your deeper state of soul. Let God reach inside you and purge the flotsam. Let him secure your heart and restore your joy with the sacred well-being that arises from his intimate companionship.

Waiting Well: Joseph Guards His Integrity

Joseph was a seventeen-year-old kid when his father, Jacob, confirmed his status as the favored son by giving him the legendary multicolored coat. He foolishly fed the fires of jealousy that raged within his eleven brothers by telling them of his dreams of grandeur, literal dreams he'd been having. He described how he'd seen his brothers' sheaves of grain bowing down to his. And then there was the dream where the sun, the moon, and eleven stars bowed down to him. Joseph was many things, but subtle was not one of them.

Although Joseph was young and lacked wisdom, the calling on his life was real and powerful. He was destined for greatness, chosen to rule. The anticipation of his destiny played with his imagination; the future was bright. But…he had no clue that his destiny lay thirteen difficult years ahead of him.

I can only imagine the terror that pummeled his senses as his brothers debated whether to kill him or sell him into slavery. His desperate pleas were coldly mocked as he was bound and dragged mercilessly away by his new masters. As his homeland receded in the distance, his destiny seemed to evaporate in the desert winds. And if not for his integrity, it would have!

From his years of faithful service in Potiphar's house to the years spent in prison after being falsely accused, Joseph was sustained by remembrance, gratitude, and vigilance. By serving wholeheartedly in every position he held, he demonstrated that he had not forgotten who he was or who God was for him. When tempted to exploit his position as chief steward and accept the sexual advances of Potiphar's wife, Joseph acknowledged with gratitude the favor of God that had elevated him to that position (see Genesis 39:7–9). He was vigilant for divine appointments, knowing that God could use him in any setting. In this way he saw the opportunity to interpret the dreams of Pharaoh's officials (see Genesis 40:6–22). He remembered that God had gifted him with dreams and operated in that confidence.

For all the injustice he endured—and he experienced far more than most of us will—this was not a beaten man. He chose not to throw away his destiny through immorality nor plummet to the depths of anger, cynicism, or discouragement. Instead, he leaned on his integrity and waited well.

Thirteen years later his endurance was rewarded with an unprecedented ascent to power. Yes, he was created to rule! And ten years later he saw the precise fulfillment of his original prophetic dream as his family gathered in Egypt to bow down before him. Because he was a man of character. A man of integrity.

Strategic Scribblings

Journaling Strategy No. 8: Leverage your integrity
through remembrance, gratitude, and vigilance.

Write down your thoughts on integrity. Think about how your integrity has been both tested and strengthened through waiting. List specific examples of remembrance, gratitude, and vigilance that seem to bear upon your current season of waiting.

_____

_____

_____

_____

Chapter Nine

Finding Time to Wait

Simple Tactics for Your First Sabbatical

> The biggest reason I have shunned silence
> and solitude is so that I don't have to face
> the most critical, demanding,
> and difficult person in my life: me.
> —FIL ANDERSON[1]

It was day one of forty, and all was not well. Already Kellie and I were irritated with each other, not to mention the effects of withdrawal from coffee, magazines, and a handful of other diversions. And it was only a few hours into my New Year's Sabbatical. Yep, one big spiritual high in the making. It seems that raising the bar on your spiritual journey carries the risk of the bar's falling on you!

Not to worry, though. Any effort we undertake to seek God's face and make room for more of him in our lives is certain to crash into obstacles. The challenge—and the adventure—comes in navigating the obstacle course. One of the challenges we encounter in our seasons of waiting is that *time itself feels like an enemy.* Oddly, the truth is just the opposite. When we're waiting, time is one of our best friends.

This is a great time to take a Sabbatical, a period of time set apart for drawing near to God for a specific purpose. Sabbaticals are often thought to be the sole domain of graying professors and robed clergy, but Sabbaticals are far too awesome to be overlooked by the rest of us.

I can almost hear your thoughts: *What can he be thinking? Who has the time to stop and just do nothing?*

The short answer: all of us.

The length of a Sabbatical is flexible and closely related to what you have faith for right now. It can be a morning or a long weekend or a month or a year…simply depending on what you want to accomplish and how much room you're willing to make for God. The point is to intentionally make space for the one thing that is most important so you can engage the other important things in your life from that place of divine partnership.

It makes perfect sense that waiting seasons are prime times for taking Sabbaticals. First, it's already a time when God has you on the shelf, so to speak, to prepare you for a coming engagement with destiny. Not really on the shelf, though. More like on the workbench. So there is a natural desire within you (and an invitation from God) to catch a glimpse of the particular work of preparation he is involved in. And second, waiting seasons are frequently times when you're facing fewer demands—either in the physical world or the spiritual or both. And this opens up a unique window of opportunity to make more room for God.

I'm not saying you're not busy. We're all busy! It's the default setting in modern America. Perhaps you've chosen to swim against that current and simplify your life. Regardless, taking time away from already full schedules always involves some difficulty, but simply put, it's worth the effort. The really important things always are. And if you'll take my dare and give a Sabbatical a try, I think you'll agree.

What exactly is a Sabbatical? And just how do you take one? Good questions. The concept of Sabbatical is an extrapolation from the biblical idea (and command) of the Sabbath, God's direction that we set aside every seventh day for rest and worship. As *Nelson's Illustrated Bible Dictionary* puts it, "The Sabbath is a means by which man's living pattern imitates God's (see Exodus 20:3–11). Work is followed by rest."[2] God originated this rhythm in creating the world.

God expanded the Sabbath principle in the life of the Jewish nation in a couple of ways, introducing the Sabbatical Year and the Year of Jubilee. The former was God's directive not only to make every seventh *day* holy but also to make every seventh *year* holy. In this seventh year, there was to be no cultivation of the soil; whatever harvest sprung up on its own was to be enjoyed and shared but not stored. The land was given a break. Also, debts were cancelled, and the entire year was understood as a time of unique rest and thanksgiving for him who is our Rest!

"The spirit of the sabbatic year is that of the weekly Sabbath. The rest that the land was to keep in the seventh year was not to increase its fruitfulness by lying fallow or merely to be a time of recreation for laboring men and beasts, needful and useful as that may be. It was rather to afford true spiritual rest and quickening, with their attendant life and blessing."[3]

The Year of Jubilee was an extension of this principle, except that it occurred after every seven series of seven years—in other words, every fiftieth year.[4]

Do you think God is trying to make a point here? These laws were not random manifestations of executive might. The author of Hebrews used the Sabbath as the symbol of our salvation (see 4:1–11), and Jesus himself reaffirmed its validity and Kingdom role in the life of the New Testament believer (see Mark 2:27). Since God's intention in this matter bears so much weight, let's consider how to incorporate its truth into our own lives.

A Sabbatical Plan

Don't be intimidated! We're going to take this lofty idea and make it practically accessible for any person and within any parameters. You can use the organizational guidelines in this chapter as a template to make your Sabbatical both exciting and fulfilling. After laying out these ideas conceptually, I'll offer perspectives and illustrations from my own experience.

Purpose

If you're not clear on what your Sabbatical is about, then chances are good you won't find it a satisfying experience. In your planning, give serious thought and prayer to what your soul hungers for. Answer Jesus' question to the blind man: "What do you want me to do for you?" (Luke 18:41). Though your need may feel as overwhelmingly obvious as that man's need for sight, it's important to verbalize it.

Your purpose could be centered around the need for specific direction or guidance. Or it could simply be born out of a desire for more of God in your life. It could be anchored in a specific project he has given you to accomplish. For example, God could be moving you into a new ministry and has called you to spend a week with him in preparation. Before you embark on the quest, take time to get equipped, beginning with crafting a short one- or two-sentence statement of purpose. Then commit your purpose to paper.

Logistics

How long should your Sabbatical last? And should it be time spent alone, with your spouse, or with a small group? Where should it be?

Your purpose for taking the Sabbatical initially will determine the parameters for how long, with whom, and where. If this adventure is about reading a book on leadership and seeking God's guidance in becoming a more effective leader in your home, then you probably don't need a month. On the other hand, if you're considering quitting your job, moving across the country, and relaunching your life in a new direction, then you probably want to spend more than a day or two. *(Oh wait, I think I did that!)*

In terms of *who*, Sabbaticals can be effective when done alone, as a couple, as a family, or as a small community of friends, extended family, or teammates. Just make sure your purpose is consistent with whom you choose to invite on the Sabbatical; otherwise, you'll frustrate the goal.

Where is simply a question of finding a location that is financially and geographically accessible and is conducive to your purpose. You can use a hotel, a vacation house, a retreat center, or a campground. You can even use your own home, although that is sometimes tougher. For a one-day or partial-day Sabbatical, choose a park, a secluded room, a friend's empty house, your church, or your car. The important things are to know what is likely to distract you and to avoid them.

I almost always prefer to go to the mountains. The two-hour drive allows me to disconnect from my responsibilities and activities and really focus on spiritual things. I love the drive, I love being alone, and I love my granddad's old mountain house. The fact that it is quiet and in a beautiful setting is a wonderful complement to my usual Sabbatical purpose.

Other logistical challenges can include taking time off from work, finding people to shoulder your responsibilities while you're gone, arranging childcare (if that applies), providing for pets, and so forth. Of course, the longer your Sabbatical the more complex the arrangements. But don't be put off by the details; no matter what it takes, the benefit will outweigh the investment. If you surrender to the flow of the status quo, your life will bear nothing more than status-quo results. God-sized results come from setting God-sized goals!

Goals

From your statement of purpose, list three to five specific goals that connect directly to your purpose. These can be written as questions—inquiries that you have of God—or as items you want to receive from God. The key to effective goals is to make them specific and measurable: you need to be able to determine when your goal has been reached. So while your purpose can be stated in more ethereal terms (a greater sense of God's presence and involvement in your life, for instance), distill your goals down to clearly defined issues.

To be sure, God will enlarge upon your goals as you spend intentional time with him. And during your season of listening, it is pretty certain that he will give you answers to questions you didn't know to ask. At the same time, he will perhaps intimate that some of your questions aren't really as imperative as you had thought. Still, a thoughtful list of goals will help you prepare to meet with him on purpose.

Sample goals might include completing a word study on servanthood, getting an answer on whether to accept a job offer, developing a list of ways to be a better spouse, or hearing God's thoughts on a difficult relationship. Your goals might be focused on issues of profession and calling, on home and family, on inner spiritual issues or ministry opportunities. They might include a smattering of all those areas. The point is that you sense God has something to say to you if you are willing to come away and make space for him!

This is a good time to establish a central perspective. We don't go to God the way we go to the Internet. He is not a divine search engine, ready to spit out information at the click of a mouse. We go to God because he is the Lover of our souls, because life finds meaning only within the circumference of his arms, and because destiny is not an impersonal decree but rather the most intimate collection of our Father's desires, personally conveyed from his heart to ours.

So it's okay to have requests, petitions, and questions of our heavenly Father—he invites them. And although he doesn't answer every question or prayer the way we expect, he always opens a wide avenue to his heart and the treasures of his house.

Now as we develop our organizational plan, we want to think about the primary channels of access to God and his treasures.

Essentials

From your set of goals, begin to consider and define the components you know are necessary to this time of Sabbatical. Essentials might include prayer, Bible study, reading, fasting, solitude and silence, community and discussion, journaling. There are many good tools to draw from as you anticipate your special time with

God. I find it helpful, however, to distinguish between activities that are essential to your quest and those that are merely enhancing. Keep this time simple and focused.

Enhancers

This is where you identify the components of your Sabbatical that will enhance your communion with God. The difference between essentials and enhancers is that the latter are negotiable—you can experiment to find out whether they do indeed draw you to the heart of God. Some activities are essential for one season, optional for another, and at other times simply irrelevant. It's good to know which is which.

That way you don't labor, for instance, reading through the book of Isaiah when the presence of God awaits you in silent meditation; conversely, you may spend hours in prayer over matters that God has addressed thoroughly in a new book that he is urging you to read. This is why a bit of preparation goes a long way toward a successful, purposeful Sabbatical with God.

Hindrances

Stating your Sabbatical purpose, solving logistics, setting goals, identifying essentials and enhancers—all of these are about how to obtain God's heart during this focused season of listening. In all these things, we are adding to our lives—adding spiritual activities, spiritual attention, and emotional focus. But of course, it's not as though you had all these blocks of empty time you were wondering how to fill. In order to add things, you have to move out other things. So your Sabbatical strategy is this: listen to God by removing unnecessary noise.

Even if you have developed a remarkable list of spiritual goals and activities, it's always easier to add than to subtract. Figuring out what you *aren't* going to do is almost more important than what you will do...because opening up space in your soul and your schedule is so foreign to our programming.

Open space in your soul is the necessary setting for an effective Sabbatical. This is why, before going any further in the planning process, you need to identify the things that would likely hinder your purpose and goals. This is the time to be ruthless. Simplify your life so that for this brief time it gets as narrow as possible. The space you create will amplify everything you are making room for—the voice of God, intimacy with God, wisdom from God, the study of things on God's heart.

Strategy No. 9:
Hear God's voice by removing unnecessary noise.

Consider this list of hindrances that most often interfere with hearing God during a Sabbatical: television, movies, the Internet, e-mail, magazines, newspapers, catalogs, shopping, comfort food, hobbies, sports, certain people, certain activities. While your set of hindrances will be unique to you, these are common categories of things that have a dulling or distracting effect. Those are what you want to avoid.

Comfort foods, as well as comfort activities, feed us emotionally. Maybe it's coffee or desserts or soap operas. One of the ways you can identify this category is to ask, *When I've had a long, hard day and I feel like treating myself, what do I do or eat?* These are usually legitimate things, not bad things. But because they have the ability to sate us emotionally, they compete with the Holy Spirit and become hindrances to the Sabbatical dynamic. For now, set them aside as a type of fasting.

Fasting itself is an ancient, proven, and biblical discipline that will enhance your Sabbatical experience. It isn't fun, but it's usually not as hard as we think it will be. The benefit from fasting—whether it's from food in general or television or shopping—is that it pulls the veneer off our souls and exposes what's underneath. The more you strip away, the more potent the dynamic. People frequently become irritable, impatient, and even angry as their body and/or soul gets purged from common habits. Sleep, food, sex, entertainment—all of these can sate us with pleasure and mask the soul issues that God wants to reveal and speak to. The things that come to the surface when we're fasting are often the things God wants to address.

Strategy

Now that we've clarified purpose, logistics, goals, essentials, enhancers, and hindrances, it's time to lay a strategy. The strategy for a one-day Sabbatical might be as simple as spending the morning in a prayerful hike and the afternoon in meditative journaling. For a multiple-day Sabbatical, there might be a spiritual theme for each day, reinforced by specific activities related to that theme.

A Sabbatical that runs for several weeks might have weekly

themes and activities—like the one I'm on right now. In just a minute, I'll show you how I broke down my purpose and goals into weekly themes. Strategizing your getaway will help you schedule your time and stay true to your purpose. These special seasons are too precious to let them get diluted.

COMMUNITY DURING SABBATICAL

During my current Sabbatical, I discovered the significance of community in these times—which is important even if you're planning a season of solitude. First, I didn't prepare very well for this particular event and, as a result, wound up spending a good bit of the Sabbatical itself replanning and recasting my vision and strategy.

Several months ago I began considering the idea of taking the first forty days of the new year as a time to renew my intimacy with God and seek his will. Although I casually mentioned the idea to Kellie, I didn't ask for her input or ideas. Naively, as it turns out.

For one thing, if you are married, you can't plan any kind of Sabbatical that exceeds a day without significant input and contribution from your spouse. The logistics alone require that. Even more, though, it needs to be addressed up front whether this is a me-thing or an us-thing. In our case, as the time neared, Kellie wanted to join me in the Sabbatical but hadn't had much chance to give input. The opportunity to build our unity became part of our essential purpose, but we had to backtrack on the planning and rebuild it together.

The first place that community comes to bear upon taking a Sabbatical is in the family itself. It's vital to incorporate the wisdom and perspective of your mate, even if he or she will not be directly involved. This is a safeguard against our own blind spots and a chance to tap the tremendous wealth of insight God has placed in your spouse. As a wise friend once told me, if you're married, half of everything God intends to say to you will come through your spouse. The smart man or woman listens carefully and expectantly to hear God speak in this way.

The next place that community comes to bear upon Sabbaticals is among close friends. There is a quality of friendship that allows us to share life together with a small band of like-minded comrades who are willing to invest their time and affections to enrich and be enriched in the daily rush of life. In the modern world this experience of community is rare, but fortunately a hunger for it is taking root among Christians who desire more of a Kingdom life. This type of living results in an interconnectedness that amplifies the spiritual growth of one person throughout the entire community. This, then, opens a wonderful door of opportunity—the chance to have close friends deeply involved in your Sabbatical, even when they're not present.

The process of including your community in the preparation, intention, experience, and evaluation of your time with God offers rich resources in many ways. People who are completely committed to your destiny in God are uniquely qualified to offer wisdom and prayer and accountability throughout the experience. If this vein of thinking makes you slightly uncomfortable, then it merely proves you are an American with all the attendant leanings toward independence and isolation. These leanings, however, run contrary to Kingdom life and will constrict your growth. They are rightly resisted.

My Sabbatical Plan

By way of example, I thought I'd share the organizational plan for my current Sabbatical to encourage you in the pursuit of your own.

Purpose

This is the purpose statement that Kellie and I created: to renew our intimacy with God, to seek his direction for us in the coming year, to increase our unity and spiritual authority together, and to make substantial progress in writing my new book. I realize this purpose statement appears rather large and disjointed, but it has actually worked well. These four purposes proved to be tightly knit together so that each contributed to the other.

Logistics

I originally chose forty days as the duration because of a popular devotional book we planned to use on our Sabbatical. But after the first day that book didn't seem relevant to our larger purpose, so we ditched it. Still, the forty-day time frame felt right, and we kept that. Because forty days is a long time, we weren't able to unplug entirely from normal life—the kids still had school, and I still had commitments to speak and lead worship. Nevertheless, wherever possible we rearranged our schedule to accommodate our goals, cut loose unnecessary activities, and punctuated those weeks with trips to the mountains.

Goals

(1) For Kellie and me to work through the *3000-Mile Marriage Tuneup* that I had developed as a four-week devotional; (2) to work out our personal and ministry calendar for the year; (3) to write "crafted prayers" (Graham Cooke's term) for each member in my family and inner community; and (4) to complete writing half of my book. In addition to these broader goals, I had a couple of specific questions of God that I was seeking answers to.

Essentials

(1) Extended daily times of prayer and discussion as a couple; (2) regular blocks of time for me to think and pray and write; and (3) fasting—from food on certain days and from other hindrances throughout.

Enhancers

(1) Exercise, (2) journaling, and (3) reading two key books. While I mentioned earlier that sports or hobbies can be a distraction, I knew ahead of time that the discipline of regular exercise was going to be an important enhancer for this time of Sabbatical. For Kellie

and me, that meant three days a week at the gym to lift weights and do cardio machines. In addition, my son and I did tae kwon do on alternating days. That level of physical focus seemed to reinforce the season of spiritual focus for us.

Journaling, a powerful practice that I never seem to maintain consistently, did not come easily for me. But rather than force it, I channeled much of the same dynamic into my book writing and going through the devotional workbook with Kellie. And that's okay. Rather than push for every planned component, follow the flow of life.

Reading books was another key piece of my Sabbatical time and structure, although not entirely as planned. The one book I had planned to read, I did not read. Two other books, however—one from the church world and one from the business world—have proved to be a perfect match for this season.

Hindrances

Of the list of hindrances that I offered earlier in this chapter, I chose to eliminate almost all of those distractions. My soul only allows for a very limited focus, so in general I have to guard my attention and activities. But for this block of time, I set aside two of my comfort foods, along with movies (probably my favorite distraction). But the single biggest soul food that I knew I was supposed to fast from might surprise you: e-mail.

Truth is, I love e-mail. It's efficient and relational, allowing me to stay connected with many people whom I wouldn't (but probably should) pick up the phone to call. But for myself, I'm discovering there is a more subtle and pathological influence at work with e-mail. I find myself checking my in-box compulsively twenty times a day, from the moment I awake until right before I get in bed. When there are a lot of messages, I get a bit of a rush. *There's mail for me! Somebody likes me and needs me. Maybe they want me to go speak somewhere. I must be important if I have twenty new e-mails.*

Although Kellie had been sounding words of warning, it took the Sabbatical finally to flush out my e-mail addiction. And with wisdom and self-control, I will be healthier in my soul as a result. That is part of the power of fasting—you voluntarily remove a good thing from your life and then take a blood-pressure reading. Was it hard to do without that thing? Do you miss it? How much do you miss it? This is a valuable reality check for the soul.

Strategies

Working with a multiweek time frame, I found it helpful to focus on a different theme every week. Week one was general soul preparation; week two was marriage and family; week three is (currently) writing and ministry; week four will be scheduling the year; week five will be worship and intimacy. After defining this, I had to rework my daily schedule extensively to make additional room for time with Kellie and time for writing. We renewed our commitment toward consistent bedtimes and wakeup times—both of which tend to drift.

So far I feel more connected with Jesus, more connected in my marriage, and well on my way toward my direction for the year. And so can you. This is the courage and reward of self-discovery, which leads us to God-discovery…and vice versa. This is the beauty of Sabbaticals.

Don't allow the busyness of your life to deter you. Most of us have demanding environments at home and work. Young professionals are pressured for long hours. Single moms face unique challenges. But the harder it is to break away, the more we need it! And the more our lives and waiting seasons will be transformed.

WAITING WELL: JESUS TAKES TIME TO SEEK THE FATHER'S WISDOM

Among the biblical characters who seized intentional seasons for prayer and listening, one stands out: Jesus. Although he was God himself, he lived in such communion with the Trinity that prayer was as natural as breath. Still, there were a few unique points in time where Jesus sensed a special need for focused communion with his Father, and off he would go to spend a night's "Sabbatical" on a mountainside.

Though several such incidents are mentioned in the Gospels (and there were almost certainly more that were not mentioned), I'll focus on one account that is quite brief: "One of those days Jesus went out to a mountainside to pray, and spent the night praying to God" (Luke 6:12). Several details are noteworthy: Jesus was alone, he chose a mountain for this intimate time with God, and his fellowship with the Father spanned the ten or twelve hours of a night.

But the larger question is why did Jesus need time in prayer? I have a general answer and a specific one. The general answer comes from Jesus' explanation in John 5:19–20:

> I tell you the truth, the Son can do nothing by himself; he
> can do only what he sees his Father doing, because whatever
> the Father does the Son also does. For the Father loves the
> Son and shows him all he does.

In general, Jesus operated out of a deep communion with his Father so that every word and deed of the Son was in complete harmony with the Father's will. The intimacy and interdependence they shared fueled everything Jesus did. I'm convinced it was times of coming away from his normal world that allowed Jesus to connect so deeply and purposefully with God the Father. If we intend to live in the center of what God is doing, then we, too, must make room to listen and watch so the Father may show us all he is doing.

But the context opens up a more specific issue as back story to Jesus' night-long Sabbatical. It is not accidental that he chose that particular moment to get away with God. This Sabbatical came during a time when Jesus' public miracles were accelerating the level of conflict he was experiencing with the Pharisees. The escalating confrontations appear to have begun in Luke 5 when Jesus healed the paralytic and, more inflammatory than that, forgave the man's sins. Shortly thereafter, the Pharisees pressed him on the issue of fasting.

But the heat really picked up in two confrontations over regulations of the Law, producing a furor of hatred as the Pharisees began plotting to harm Jesus. Precisely at this moment, Jesus slipped away to get quiet before his Father and listen for fresh instruction. And that instruction came!

Immediately upon Jesus' return the following morning, he launched the plan that surely came from that intimate fellowship the night before: he chose twelve men from among all his followers to be uniquely trained and equipped to multiply his ministry on earth. Can you see it? The sheer brilliance of God's wisdom is astounding—and it's the same wisdom he will unlock for us as we break away from normal life to be with him in Sabbatical seasons.

Strategic Scribblings

Journaling Strategy No. 9:
Hear God's voice by removing unnecessary noise.

Put this strategy into motion by planning your next (or perhaps first) Sabbatical for a time within the next three months. Make it a day, a weekend, a week—you choose.

Purpose: _____

Logistics: _____

Goals:_____

Essentials:_____

Enhancers:_____

Hindrances:_____

Strategies:_____

Other Sabbatical Notes:_____

_____

_____

_____

_____

_____

_____

_____

Chapter Ten

Never Let Go of Your Destiny

A Longing Fulfilled Is a Tree of Life

> Never give in—never, never, never, never,
> in nothing great or small, large or petty,
> never give in except to convictions
> of honour and good sense. Never yield
> to force; never yield to the apparently
> overwhelming might of the enemy!
> —WINSTON CHURCHILL[1]

The early morning sun warmed the back of my neck as I watched the spinning blur of Kevin's back tire and the hypnotic pumping of his hamstrings just a few feet in front of my bicycle. I was tucked into the cycling line just behind my brother-in-law as four of us churned together toward our destination—still seventy miles away. This was my first tour, and after an hour in the saddle, I was beginning to settle into a happy rhythm as the pack snaked quickly, purposefully down the rural highway.

It was a small race—not even a race, really. Just a long ride to raise money for diabetes research. But having trained alone, I was new to the group-riding dynamic. I knew that when a group rides together, the lead rider opens a passage in the wind, and the other riders draft in his wake…until the leader needs a break and peals off to the back so a new leader can pull for a while.

There was a silent joy in the interplay among us. Kevin and I found ourselves in the front pack, working with two riders we'd never met before. But the four of us worked together in perfect harmony, riding faster and farther than I'd ever ridden before—all because of the team's synergy. With thirty miles behind us, the yellow line beneath me was a hypnotic ribbon. The wind whistled in my ears, and I shook out my hands to keep them from going numb on the bars. At thirty-seven miles we reached the bottom of Pilot Mountain, our halfway point. Then came the big climb… two and a half miles up a grade that reached 15 percent.

Within moments we had dropped to our lowest gear ratio… and realized that it wasn't low enough! I stood up in my saddle to gain extra leverage but quickly figured out that I couldn't stand all the way up the mountain. My crank was turning just fast enough to maintain my balance; in truth, it was the fear of falling over that kept my legs straining forward. In desperation I began to weave back and forth on the road, getting minor relief on every other stroke as I cut the grade angle ever so slightly. Expending every ounce of energy, I finally crested the top and looked out over the dramatic view all around—forest, punctuated by fields and farmhouses a thousand feet below the rocky cliffs.

The forty-mile-per-hour downhill threw me onto a razor edge between terror and utter delight as I worked the switchbacks left and then right. But as the rush receded at the bottom, it dawned on me that my legs were pretty well shot, and thirty miles still awaited me. As soon as we hit the first upward swell in the road, I knew I had no staying power left for climbs. Kevin would stick with me, but we let the other two cyclists know I was dragging and that they should push ahead. "No," they assured me. "We've come this far together; we're going to take it all the way together."

I was strangely warmed but also mystified by their loyalty. Cyclists are a competitive lot and fiercely independent. But these two seemed to value the team dynamic, so I tucked back into the line, and we churned forward. On the straightaways I could maintain a decent pace, slower than our earlier pace but still respectable. When it came to the hills, I fell back, but the other three moderated their pace, and we stayed together. Forty miles. Fifty miles. The gray river of road sparkled and spun off into the distance, but now there were only two realities for me: keeping my front tire a foot or two behind the next bike and watching the road for potholes and gravel.

As we drew nearer the city, the climbs grew more frequent and more steep. *I can't do this,* the rational part of my brain said. *If I'm going to make it at all, I'm going to have to cut my pace in half.* But they wouldn't let me. Our commitment to one another had grown now—shared pain does that. One guy's chain came off, and we all stopped until it was back on.

We were about fifteen miles out when an amazing thing started to happen. Brian was the strongest rider in our pack, and he had been in the lead for some time. In fact, he would keep the point position for the rest of the ride. I was in the number-two spot, and Brian was taking it on himself to drag me across the finish line. Yelling words of encouragement, he urged me forward. *I don't have it! It's just not there,* my mind screamed. But Brian yelled louder: "Get your butt in gear! You can do this!"

We hit the next hill, and my quads felt like jelly. They rejected my urgent pleas to keep the pressure on the pedals. Brian pulled out and coasted back beside me. As I labored for each rotation, he planted his right hand on my back and pushed...yes, *pushed* me up that hill! Though I felt slightly embarrassed, my gratitude was larger. "Thanks, dude," I squeaked out as my breath returned at the crest of the hill. But on the next hill, there he was again—pulling energy out of me that I knew wasn't there. Again he reached out and gave me a ten-second push to give my feeble legs a spot of relief. "Give me another gear," he urged quietly. "You've got it now!"

For ten or fifteen miles, to my mind-bending amazement, Brian reached out and pushed me up every hill. Gasping, groaning, everything was in pain—my rear, my shoulders, my hands, my back. Yet in my trancelike condition, his words of hope and confidence echoed through my head and kept me moving with the pack. The hills blurred together in an endless cadence as I kept thinking each was the final hill I could pedal, even with Brian's help. And then there it was, the left turn and the finish line. Somehow the four of us had regained the lead position, but just before we crossed over, Brian pulled out from his lead spot...so I would cross the line first. *What kind of a guy is this?*

My eyes blurred with tears as my feet slowed their exhausted circumference. The weight of what I had done—and what had been done for me—washed over my soul. The sheer grace of it all tangled my mind with confused wonder. *Why would a stranger help me so much and then, to cap it off, give me the honor of crossing the finish line first?* It just wouldn't compute. I struggled to find words of thanks, but they seemed inadequate. I hoped that this mysterious cyclist knew what it meant to me, what he had done.

Strategy No. 10:
Never give up.

Before the race I had told a friend about the compelling motivation behind my riding this tour. I felt the physical exertion of riding the seventy-mile course was a tangible parallel to my spiritual journey just then. But I wasn't prepared for my encounter with Brian; this experience of personal perseverance, empowering grace, and practical community will mark me for years.

Our waiting seasons—yours and mine—are not time trials but

tours. Not a sprint but a test of endurance. We have to go the distance. Never give up.

Getting Beyond Ourselves

A year ago my literary agent was hammering out a book contract with my soon-to-be publisher. The main terms had been agreed upon, but the actual verbiage of the contract dragged on for months. *Good grief,* I thought, *how long can it take to tweak a few paragraphs?* But later my agent explained that, since this was the first contract between his agency and this particular publisher, they were carving out new territory. The waiting I was experiencing was not only for my benefit but also for the benefit of other authors who would come after me. Their journey would be much shorter because I had plowed the way for them.

Do you think it could be that way for us, too? That the things we carve out in the hot, sweaty, interminable desert could benefit not only us but those who come after us? I think they do, and here's why.

Our seasons of waiting help our friends, those who walk through the desert with us. Although it's not their desert, they get to learn from our struggles. There is also tremendous benefit to our children. Everything we learn we get to pass along to them, both in the natural and in the spiritual realms. And then there are the people God will bring into our sphere of influence: God redemptively engineers our paths to cross those who need what we have learned…and vice versa. In this way, the Kingdom of God is built with exponential grace!

SECURITY IN MYSTERY

As the grace of God molds us during times of waiting, I have come to believe that part of his intent is to establish within us a higher level of ease and familiarity with mystery. Although we search for the meaning behind certain events and circumstances, we don't place our security in understanding things completely. Instead, we rest in a wonderful, unfathomable, and mysterious relationship with the King of the universe, the Lover of our souls.

Every soul has to be set free from the compulsion to try to control his little world. No matter how talented and capable we are, if we try to control life, we're bound for frustration. In fact, God sets out to frustrate us in our efforts to run things. "This is the point at which God most feels like our enemy," says author John Eldredge. "It seems at times that he will go to any length to thwart the very thing we most deeply want."[2] Why is that? Because waiting is all about *process*. And we can understand process only in hindsight... if at all.

This reality forces us into the blessing of relinquishing control. God wants us to know and believe in the deepest part of our being that he is trustworthy. He draws us to rest in the embrace of his control and goodness. To rest in mystery. As Gerald May writes:

> The dark night—indeed all of life—is nothing other than the story of a love affair: a romance between God and the human soul that liberates us to love one another.... The Beloved is endless Mystery, always beyond our capacity to

comprehend. Therefore, if we have a choice, it is best for all of us to hold both our beliefs and disbeliefs lightly.[3]

That scares me a little, but it also frees me. Figuring out God is the product of eternity, but loving our Mysterious Maker is the product of now. The goal is not so much to build a creed, a neat box of carefully arranged words to make us secure in knowledge. Instead, the goal is to build trust, a security without boundaries...a security anchored in a Person. This is the opportunity of waiting well.

THE STORY GOES ON

As you read this final chapter, you might be expecting a resolution to the story. Perhaps you thought that after nine chapters on waiting, I'd close with a chapter describing how great it is to finally lay hold of your destiny—God's reward for those who have waited well.

If that's what you were hoping for, I'm sorry to disappoint you. I'm still waiting.

God has conveyed a destiny to Kellie and me through many people and events over the last eight or ten years, and while there is movement, the manifestation of our destiny still awaits us. A year ago, when I began writing this book, I hoped that the finish line for our waiting would emerge before I had to deliver the manuscript. I hoped that I'd have a glorious story to tell of hope awakened, of hope challenged, of hope fulfilled.

I don't.

But maybe that's not all bad. Perhaps *not* having a nice, tidy ending to the story is precisely that which validates my challenge to you to wait well. It's easy to talk about the benefits and opportunities of waiting after it's over! But to be fully convinced of the good heart of the Father and to relish the journey even in the midst of waiting somehow feels more valuable, more authentic, more accessible, more true.

This book is more about a new perspective than it is a wealth of new information. And I find that strangely appropriate. Waiting seasons aren't so much about digging up new knowledge as they are about developing new character. About moving truth from our head to our heart to our feet—walking out the truth we know when circumstances are tough. That kind of perseverance brings enormous reward! But because of the disorienting nature of waiting times, we desperately need something or someone to remind us of what we know and to help us hold on to it and not let go. I hope this book can be such a friend.

Don't ever let go of your destiny! Your God-breathed future is a deposit of heaven on earth and should be treasured until it appears in its fullness. And appear it will.

A Longing Fulfilled...

We've heard the wisdom of Solomon: "Hope deferred makes the heart sick" (Proverbs 13:12). Now here is the wonderful ending to that verse: "But a longing fulfilled is a tree of life." Not all our longings are fulfilled yet, but some of them are. The longings that touch us deeply are placed there by our Maker. Graham Cooke says, "During those times you sit in the presence of God and your heart sighs for Him, what is it you are sighing for? Understand that your sigh originated in His heart.... You cannot have a desire or longing for God that He did not put there."[4]

Our deepest longing is for the Lover himself, and that is one longing that he intends to satisfy continually, whether we find ourselves in a waiting season or whether that season has ended and we are thrust forth into destiny. I expect that, in one sense, waiting never really ends. God is always enlarging our soul, always enlarging our view of him and what he wants to do through us. So just as soon as one element of divine intention is realized in our lives, it is replaced by another, bigger, grander invitation into destiny.

Still, "there is a time for everything, and a season for every activity under heaven" (Ecclesiastes 3:1). Some seasons are defined by waiting while others are shaped more by doing. Embrace the longings, and embrace the fulfillment of longings. And let that tree of life well up inside you until it overflows.

It was some months ago that a fresh realization hit me...*I am living the life I want to live.* Yes, even with many promises still hanging out there beyond my grasp, I am living the life God intends for me. Right now I get to write, I get to share my experiences with groups of people, I get to lead worship and enjoy the divine Presence. My life is good! And so is yours when you look with God's perspective.

A Tenacious Favor

Earlier this year I read a tremendous book called *Good to Great,* a book ostensibly about managing your business but really about managing your life. Among many insightful principles, one stands out: "Retain absolute faith that you can and will prevail in the end, regardless of the difficulties, and at the same time confront the most brutal facts of your current reality, whatever they might be."[5] Our ability to wait well requires both of these elements to work in tandem—absolute honesty about our current conditions combined with an unswerving commitment to God's promised future. Realism plus tenacity equals breakthrough.

So while we might be tempted to label our lives *Terrible to Tolerable,* I believe that God's work in us can aptly be called *Good to Great.* I can say that with confidence, because we live under a tenacious favor. No matter what challenges and enemies surround you, if you look carefully you will see filaments of God's favor woven throughout your life.

God's favor is an amazing thing—seemingly too good to apply to the likes of us. *I mess up so often,* our hearts tell us. *God can't bless me unless I do things the right way.* We are quick to believe this lie. But crucial to navigating the desert successfully is understanding the heart of the Father toward us. God favors his children. His favor toward us exceeds our wildest imaginings. It is unrelated to our doing everything right (we can't anyway), and it breathes hope into every season of waiting.

Waiting Well: Jacob Perseveres and Enjoys Favor

Jacob's life was not an easy one. His story is filled with failure and enormous hurdles. Yet, despite his shortcomings, I appreciate and value Jacob's journey. First, his life turns upon the hinges of several defining encounters with God. Second, and more to the point, Jacob refuses to give up.

Fleeing for his life from his embittered brother, Esau, the young Jacob takes up residence with his deceitful uncle Laban and agrees to labor for seven years to win the hand of Laban's beautiful daughter Rachel. The long years pass swiftly because of Jacob's great love for Rachel. But on their wedding night, Laban pulls off an extraordinary feat and substitutes Leah, his older daughter, for Rachel. Furious at the betrayal, Jacob still agrees to work an additional seven years in exchange for his true love. Jacob knew something about waiting!

But Laban's trickery doesn't end there. And although Jacob isn't an innocent party in this shoving match, Laban continually positions Jacob to get the worst end of every arrangement. Laban changes Jacob's wages ten times over the final six years they work together. Finally, after twenty years of this, Jacob has had enough. He intends to return to his homeland in Canaan with his wives and children and flocks. Through God's protection, he does indeed return and so fulfills the promise God gave him many years earlier.

Two things allowed Jacob to endure his protracted waiting season: a persevering spirit and the favor of God. He could have bailed out and run many times during the years of servitude, but he didn't. He saw his goal and stuck to it.

It is sometimes strange to us how God can blend favor and adversity. In the midst of Jacob's obstacles and heartache, there was a very real current of favor that flowed to him. By the time he left his uncle's employ, he was immensely wealthy by every standard of measure. He had two wives, twelve children, perhaps hundreds of servants and thousands of sheep, goats, camels, donkeys, and other livestock. He had gold and silver. It seemed that the more Jacob was oppressed by people or circumstances, the more he prospered.

The favor God bestowed had nothing to do with Jacob's sterling performance. After all, Jacob was a recovering schemer and made more than his share of foolish mistakes. But he belonged to God, and God's destiny for his life would not be denied. So God taught and corrected Jacob through the many reproofs of life. And he blessed him, as he will bless us if we refuse to give up.

> So let's not allow ourselves to get fatigued doing good. At the right time we will harvest a good crop if we don't give up, or quit. (Galatians 6:9, MSG)

ENCOURAGEMENT IN WAITING WELL

Even though this book comes to a close, your waiting may continue. With all my heart I wish to help you make sense of your divine delay and come into partnership with God during this season. It's not for nothing. Rather, it is for a very important something! Your waiting well will qualify you to step into your promised future. Take a moment now to review the strategies we have covered in our time together, and let God unleash their potential in your journey. Go with God.

- Embrace the now.
- Allow the rub of waiting to confirm your larger destiny.
- Search out new paths of communion with God.
- Let adversity become the means of your success.
- Lean into your fall.
- Choose your crew well.
- Adopt the Joshua paradigm: cut off, change, and confirm.
- Leverage your integrity through remembrance, gratitude, and vigilance.
- Hear God's voice by removing unnecessary noise.
- Never give up.

Strategic Scribblings

Journaling Strategy No. 10: Never give up.

Jot down the specific areas of life in which you are tempted to let go and give up. Now open your spiritual ears and hear what Jesus wants to say to you about those areas. Write down his words of truth and encouragement and endurance. Feel his breath that warms you with new courage, wisdom, and resolve to go the distance.

Notes

Introduction: An Invitation to Intimacy

1. To read the complete story of our Sabbatical, what precipitated it, and how God changed us as a result, see my book *Soul Space* (Brentwood, TN: Integrity, 2003).

2. Kenneth Barker, ed., *The NIV Study Bible* (Grand Rapids: Zondervan, 1995), 771. See note on Job 42:7–9.

Chapter 1: Why All This Waiting?

1. Brennan Manning, *Ruthless Trust* (New York: Harper-Collins, 2000), 150.

2. The additional years listed for some of the waiting periods indicate a second period of waiting after the person received a partial fulfillment from God.

3. Not specified in Scripture; these are educated guesses.

4. Not specified in Scripture; these are educated guesses.

5. Not specified in Scripture; these are educated guesses.

6. Jesus waited approximately eighteen years from the time he was a boy debating with the experts in the Law at the Temple in Jerusalem to begin his earthly ministry by being baptized by John.

7. Henri Nouwen, *Can You Drink the Cup?* (Notre Dame, IN: Ave Maria Press, 1996), 56.

8. Manning, *Ruthless Trust*, 150.

Chapter 2: Of Giants and Grasshoppers

1. Kathy Wenzel, "Rekindle the Flame," *Smoldering Wick Newsletter,* February 15, 2004, 1. See www.smolderingwick ministries.org.

Chapter 3: Flying on Instruments

1. Sue Monk Kidd, *When the Heart Waits* (New York: Harper-Collins, 1990), 4, 10.
2. For more on this idea, see Gary Thomas, *Sacred Pathways* (Grand Rapids: Zondervan, 2000).
3. For more on this idea, see Graham Cooke, *Hiddenness and Manifestation* (Tonbridge, England: Sovereign World, 2003).

Chapter 4: Dreams for Sale

1. Graham Cooke, *The Nature of God* (Tonbridge, England: Sovereign World, 2003), 19.
2. Cooke, *The Nature of God,* 11.
3. Jim Stockdale, quoted in Jim Collins, *Good to Great* (New York: HarperCollins, 2001), 85.
4. Richard Curtis, *Notting Hill* (Universal City, CA: Universal Studios, 1999).
5. Fil Anderson, *Running on Empty* (Colorado Springs: WaterBrook, 2004), 79.
6. For more on these ideas, see Jerome Daley, *Soul Space* (Brentwood, TN: Integrity, 2003) or www.soulspace.com.

Chapter 5: I Can't Do This!

1. Tucker Ritner, "Poem of Moses." Used by permission of the poet.
2. Graham Cooke, *The Nature of God* (Tonbridge, England: Sovereign World, 2003), 22.

Chapter 6: Looking for a Yellow Submarine

1. John Lennon and Paul McCartney, "Yellow Submarine," copyright © 1966 Northern Songs, Music Sales Group, Ltd.

Chapter 7: The Night Must End

1. Julie Taymor, "Endless Night," copyright ©1997 Walt Disney Music Co.

Chapter 8: Staying Power

1. Dennis Prager, *Happiness Is a Serious Problem* (New York: HarperCollins, 1998), 59.
2. Gerald May, *The Dark Night of the Soul* (New York: HarperCollins, 2004), 1–2.
3. C. S. Lewis, *Prince Caspian* (New York: Scholastic, 1951), 79.
4. May, *The Dark Night of the Soul,* 6.

Chapter 9: Finding Time to Wait

1. Fil Anderson, *Running on Empty* (Colorado Springs: WaterBrook, 2004), 91.

2. *Nelson's Illustrated Bible Dictionary,* electronic version, s.v. "Sabbatical."

3. *New Unger's Bible Dictionary,* electronic version, s.v. "Sabbatical Year."

4. *New Unger's Bible Dictionary,* electronic version, s.v. "Year of Jubilee."

Chapter 10: Never Let Go of Your Destiny

1. Winston Churchill, from an address given at Harrow School on October 29, 1941. See a transcript of the speech online at www.winstonchurchill.org/i4a/pages/index.cfm?pageid=423.

2. John Eldredge, *The Journey of Desire* (Nashville: Nelson, 2000), 91.

3. Gerald May, *The Dark Night of the Soul* (New York: HarperCollins, 2004), 12–13.

4. Graham Cooke, *The Nature of God* (Tonbridge, England: Sovereign World, 2003), 22–23.

5. Jim Collins, *Good to Great* (New York: HarperCollins, 2001), 88.